THE

PROGRESSIVE

MOVEMENT

Advocating Social Change

The Abolitionist Movement

The Civil Rights Movement

The Environmental Movement

The Ethnic and Group Identity Movements

The Family Values Movement

The Labor Movement

The Progressive Movement

The Women's Rights Movement

REFORM MOVEMENTS
IN AMERICAN
HISTORY

THE

PROGRESSIVE
MOVEMENT

ADVOCATING SOCIAL CHANGE

Tim McNeese

CHELSEA HOUSE
PUBLISHERS
An imprint of Infobase Publishing

Cover: Progressive Party candidate Theodore Roosevelt campaigns during the 1912 presidential election.

The Progressive Movement: Advocating Social Change

Copyright © 2008 by Infobase Publishing

Chelsea House
An imprint of Infobase Publishing
132 West 31st Street
New York NY 10001

Library of Congress Cataloging-in-Publication Data
McNeese, Tim.
 The progressive movement : advocating social change / Tim McNeese.
   p. cm. — (Reform movements in American history)
 Includes bibliographical references and index.
 ISBN-13: 978-0-7910-9501-0 (hardcover)
 ISBN-10: 0-7910-9501-0 (hardcover)
 1. United States—Politics and government—1865–1933—Juvenile literature.
2. Progressivism (United States politics—History—nineteenth century—Juvenile literature. 3. Progressivism (United States politics—History—twentieth century—Juvenile literature. 4. United States—Social conditions—1865–1918—Juvenile literature. 5. Social movements—United States—History—Juvenile literature. 6. Social problems—United States—History—Juvenile literature. 7. Social change—United States—History—Juvenile literature. I. Title.
 E661.M435 2007
 324.2732'7—dc22   2007014920

Series design by Kerry Casey
Cover design by Ben Peterson

Printed in the United States of America
Bang EJB 10 9 8 7 6 5 4 3 2 1
This book is printed on acid-free paper.

CONTENTS

1

A Tragedy in New York

It was a beautiful day in New York City. The 500 employees of the Triangle Shirtwaist Company were just leaving work. It was only four-thirty in the afternoon, and out on the streets eight stories below, these garment laborers, the vast majority of them women, were about to exit the Asch Building and find a perfect Saturday waiting for them. The weather was brisk and sunny on March 25, 1911, but it was not the best part of that Saturday afternoon. It was the end of the workweek for the hundreds of workers who labored an average of 54 hours, six days a week, Monday through Saturday.

Just as the garment workers prepared to leave their work stations, all heading for the single, unlocked exit on the eighth floor, a young female worker burst into the large open work area. Out of breath, she ran to one of the few men on the floor, Samuel Bernstein, the company production manager.

"There is a fire, Mr. Bernstein!"[1] she cried out.

Bernstein and a few other male workers ran to the location of the fire and began to pour buckets of water on the blaze. They were repeating actions they had taken just a few weeks earlier when another, smaller fire had been detected in the loft factory. This time, however, the fire could not be controlled. One of the men who battled the building blaze later recalled how persistent the fire had been. The water had done no good. "It was like there was kerosene in the water," he remembered. "It just seemed to spread it."[2]

AN ACCIDENT WAITING TO HAPPEN

The 10-story Asch Building housed the Triangle Shirtwaist Company on three of its upper floors—the seventh, eighth, and ninth stories. (A shirtwaist was a woman's cotton shirt that was styled similar to a man's shirt but tailored to have a "feminine" appearance.) The Asch Building was a relatively new structure. Situated on the lower end of Manhattan Island, the 10-story building occupied the northwest corner of Green Street and Washington Place. The building still stands today more than a century later, now an academic facility of New York University. One block west was Washington Square. Buildings such as the Asch were being built throughout the city. Beginning around 1900, factory owners and other businessmen had spent $150 million on such loft factories in lower Manhattan. They were designed with safety in mind, crafted of brick or stone, and touted to be fireproof. There were approximately 500 shirtwaist and dressmaking companies scattered throughout New York City during the first decade of the twentieth century, and they employed tens of thousands of women. Each year, these seamstresses and garment workers produced $50 million worth of clothing. Despite their output, the factory owners paid workers little and constantly scrimped on working conditions, and despite the sturdy, nearly fireproof exteriors, the buildings that the garment workers labored in featured interior rooms that were framed with wood, which, in case of fire, could become tinderboxes. With few building regulations or codes (most of them were rarely, if ever, enforced), the Asch Building did not have adequate fire escapes or staircases.

Other factors made the Asch Building a ticking time bomb. The workers of the Triangle Shirtwaist Factory had never participated in a fire drill, so no one really knew what to do or where to go in case of fire. With only one door on the eighth floor, there were few options available to exit the building safely. Despite earlier fires in the Asch, there were no safety measures taken—no improvements were made to the building. The three floors that housed the Triangle Factory had access to only two narrow staircases. All but one of the doors on these floors were kept bolted shut during work hours, officially to keep workers from stealing fabric and loafing in the hallways during work hours. Other than the staircases, the only way out of the building was by two small service elevators capable of holding no more than seven or eight people. There was only one fire escape for the entire building, and it only went down to the second floor. All around the work areas on the three floors of the shirtwaist factory, "piles of cloth, tissue paper, rags, and cuttings covered the company's tables, shelves, and floors. The floors and machines were soaked with oil, and barrels of machine oil lined the walls."[3] The Triangle Shirtwaist Company was an accident waiting to happen.

Workers had recently attempted to do something about the poor conditions at the garment factory. Less than two years earlier, 200 of the workers at the Triangle Shirtwaist Factory, the majority of whom were Jewish and Italian immigrant laborers, had walked off their jobs over a long list of grievances. This was part of a widely organized series of strikes and walkouts across New York City that involved between 10,000 and 20,000 garment workers. At the peak of the citywide protest, which would come to be known as the Uprising of the Twenty Thousand, 75 percent of those who refused to return to their jobs were young women between the ages of 16 and 25. Almost all were either foreign born or

By 1910, conditions in New York's garment factories had become so abominable that many workers walked off the job in protest. The tailors pictured here were just two of the approximately 20,000 workers who participated in the New York Shirtwaist Strike that lasted from November 1909 to February 1910.

the daughters of first-generation immigrants to the United States. Eighty percent of the garment workers in New York City were women.

The workers at the Triangle Shirtwaist factory had not organized into a labor union but instead had chosen to join together under the banner of an Employees Benevolent Association. The protesting workers were upset about terrible working conditions. They labored daily in a crowded work environment, and they claimed that their factory was unsafe and a fire hazard. The air in the factory was foul, their workspaces were unsanitary, and the doors and windows of their building were nailed shut. Six days a week they worked in the garment factory and were paid little money to show for their efforts. Their bosses sometimes abused their time to an even greater extent when rush orders had to be filled. At those times, the employees were expected to work overtime or through Sunday, the only day of rest each week, without additional pay.

The walkout lasted nearly six months and did manage to yield some positive results for the garment workers. Employers generally agreed to reduce the workweek to 52 hours on average and to increase wages between 12 and 15 percent. The workers at the Triangle Shirtwaist factory did not emerge from their experience with many advantages, though, because they were not technically recognized as a labor union. Many of their workers had been replaced by strikebreakers who kept their jobs even after a settlement was reached. In many ways, those who could return to their jobs had returned to a workplace that was simply business as usual. Now those terrible work conditions had finally erupted suddenly into flames, turning the Triangle Shirtwaist factory into a deadly inferno.

DEATH WITHIN AND WITHOUT

As the flames began to spread, so did the panic among the female workers. Bernstein gave up on fighting the fire. "You can't do anything here!" he shouted to those nearest him who had battled the inferno. "Try to get the girls out!"[4]

Everywhere, the screams of the girls filled the air. Approximately 225 workers were on the eighth floor that afternoon, and they were all anxiously searching for a way out. They shouted out the names of other family members who worked in the building, including sisters and mothers, fathers and brothers. In just minutes, the fire had spread over several floors. Flames leapt out of the eighth-story windows and arced upward, entering the windows on the ninth and tenth floors. On the tenth floor were large stacks of stored cloth. On the ninth floor, panicky workers discovered that the doors to the freight elevators were locked. Soon, more than 150 workers were struggling to access the same staircase and a narrow passageway that barely measured 29 inches in width. On the tenth floor, some workers made their way up rather than down, exiting the building onto the roof. Some found their way onto the two freight elevators. As they descended, other female workers jumped into the elevator shafts onto the top of the elevators. One of the elevators stopped working after so many bodies crammed the elevator shaft. The other broke down when the electrical system malfunctioned. Only 15 minutes had passed. From the street below, bystanders gawked in horror as the upper stories of the Asch Building burned with an intense heat, the flames moving in a dance of death.

Death soon found its way to the street itself. As hundreds of people watched, girls appeared in the upper story windows only to leap to the street below. Firemen had arrived, and managed to catch some of the unfortunate fire victims in their safety nets—but only a few were saved. Many of those who jumped into the nets only managed to force the nets to the sidewalks, crushed under hurtling bodies, their falls creating "a force almost a thousand times their actual weight."[5]

Despite the destructiveness of the fire, it did not last long. Firefighters arrived fairly quickly, and within 15 minutes, firemen had the flames under control. Hundreds of workers did manage to find their way out of the burning building, only to reach the street below and become witnesses to the devastation eight stories above the street. The fire had burned for only a fraction of an hour, but, in that time, nearly 50 victims had jumped from upper-story windows to their deaths. Inside the building, firefighters would discover the burned corpses of 100 workers. The majority were Jewish workers, and all but 21 were women.

Although firefighters were quick to respond to the fire at the Triangle Shirtwaist factory in New York City's 10-story Asch Building, 146 garment workers were either burned alive or jumped to their deaths during the March 25, 1911, fire. Here, firefighters spray the upper floors of the building, which was on the corner of Greene Street and Washington Place.

Nearly a dozen were so badly burned by the fire that they were never identified. On the floor of the factory, workers would later find 14 engagement rings. Because the employees had been paid just before the fire had started, bodies were found with pay envelopes stuffed inside their clothing. Some died still holding their hard-earned wages in their hands.

After the fire, the bodies were collected in police "death wagons" and taken to a temporary morgue set up at the East 26th Street Pier. Tens of thousands of people, many of them Jews from the Lower East Side, thronged the pier, grieving as they searched for loved ones. It was a scene of emotional devastation:

> Heartbreaking scenes of recognition filled the night. A mother, discovering her daughter's body, would break down into uncontrollable wailing and have to be escorted out. A young woman, finding her sister's charred body, would simply faint. Some women completely lost control and tried to kill themselves, either by swallowing poison or by jumping off the pier. Police and onlookers stopped at least a dozen such attempts.[6]

On April 5, a mass funeral was held in Lower Manhattan. More than 100,000 people attended the tragic memorial service, many of them women workers from the Lower East Side who "marched silently in the rain for five hours to honor the Triangle dead."[7] These workers were angry and bitter. They wanted someone to pay for what had happened. One small group of women marched that day carrying a banner that read, "We demand fire protection."[8] As the march continued, the women mourners wound their way up to Washington Square Park to Fifth Avenue and onto 34th Street. Finally, they arrived at the Asch Building, the scene of the fiery devastation. There, many of those marching broke down, releasing, as one newspaper reporter wrote, "one long-drawn-out, heart-piercing cry, the mingling of thousands of voices, a cry that was perhaps the most impressive expression of human grief ever heard in this city."[9]

THE AFTERMATH OF TRAGEDY

A week after the massive funeral march, two owners of the Triangle Shirtwaist Company—Isaac Harris and Max Blanck—were indicted by a grand jury and charged with manslaughter. The trial opened in December, and much of the testimony hinged on whether the two men knew that nearly all the doors of the factory were kept locked at all times, thus making escape from the fire that fateful day difficult. When it was over, the two owners were found not guilty, because the prosecutors had not proven "beyond a reasonable doubt" that Harris and Blanck knew of the locked doors. Thus, the tragedy of the Triangle Fire was made even more tragic. The story of this horrific disaster might have ended at that point, but other influences intervened.

New York City and state officials soon launched a political campaign to right the wrongs that had led to the fire and its disastrous consequences. The state legislature established the New York Factory Investigating Commission in June 1911 to examine the working conditions that existed not only in the garment industry but in many other workplaces. State officials clearly wanted to avoid another Triangle Fire in the future. When the commission finally issued its reports later that year, legislators leapt into action, intent on making many changes in the world of industry. Between 1911 and 1915, the New York State Legislature witnessed the introduction of more than 60 bills and managed to pass all but 4 of them. The scope of this grand legislative landslide would be wide indeed. New laws were passed to create a Bureau of Fire Prevention; compulsory fire drills at work places; the installation of sprinklers in factories; an increase in the number of factory inspectors; more authority for the state's Department of Labor; a statewide workweek of 54 hours and minimum wages for women and children; a ban on night work for women; a ban on smoking in factories; improved work conditions, including better ventilation; sanitation; improved working facilities; rest periods for workers; an outlaw of child labor in tenement shops and canneries; a ban on Sunday work in factories; a program of workmen's insurance; and a law against labor of children under the age of 14.

The Triangle Shirtwaist Company Fire had caused many in New York to wake up to the horrible working conditions that its unprotected laborers had struggled under for many years. The fire had sparked the consciences of many who had merely given lip service to protecting workers. In a dazzling spectacle of legislative remorse, officials had used their power to create a better future for the previously unprotected workers of New York.

Such legislation was also spurred by other events that were taking place at that turning point in American history. A great social, political, and moral movement was engulfing the nation just as the Triangle Fire erupted on the New York urban landscape. It was a movement whose supporters advocated change for a better America, an enlightened view based on a belief that progress can only be measured by improving the lives of as many people as possible. Those who supported this new era of progress, as well as positive political and economic change, marched under the banner of a social consciousness that they called Progressivism.

2

Creating Modern America

The first and still unparalleled era of reform in the twentieth century began because of changes that took place in the United States during the last three decades of the nineteenth century. From the end of the greatest American upheaval of the 1800s—the Civil War (1861–1865)—to 1900, nearly everything changed in the United States. Much of the change was dramatic. During the days before the war began, Americans were largely farmers and ranchers, shopkeepers and small businessmen, artisans and craftsmen. After the war, a great number of Americans began to earn their living in ways that had barely made a dent in the labor force of previous generations. The United States seemed to be a nation moving ahead, growing, advancing, becoming something more to itself and to others around the world. Between 1870 and 1900, the population nearly doubled, from 39 million to 76 million. The new Americans were richer than ever before, with annual per-capita incomes increasing from $780 to nearly $1,200. Those last three decades of the nineteenth century "proved to be the exhilarating prelude to the triumphs and tragedies of the twentieth century."[10]

Much about the country and its people had changed little from earlier times. The land was still enormous and filled with vast quantities of natural resources, providing the raw materials—iron, coal, copper, oil, wood—that could be transformed into

EDUCATION FOR THE MASSES

During the decades following the American Civil War, the United States witnessed a new emphasis on an element of life that, for many, had previously been lacking—education. Schools had turned out relatively well-educated children in the United States since the Pilgrims landed at Plymouth Rock, but education had not always been made available to the vast majority of America's youth. The period from 1870 to 1900 would try to change that.

In the years after the Civil War, "school" was on its way to becoming a normal, common experience in America. Thirty-one state legislatures passed laws that made elementary school attendance compulsory, or required. Such laws dramatically changed American education. By 1898, 15 million school-age children were enrolled in the lower grades, learning the three R's (reading, writing, and arithmetic), and sometimes music or art. These schools were typically presided over by women who were the classroom teachers. By the turn of the century, kindergartens, rare in America's early years, spread rapidly.

With this new emphasis on children attending elementary schools, a natural pressure came to bear on high schools and their availability. (During the late nineteenth century, such schools were sometimes called "people's colleges.") In 1870, there were approximately 500 "high schools" in the nation; by 1900, the number had risen to more than 6,000. During the next 14 years, leading to World War I, the number of high school students increased by 250 percent! Such schools were considered important 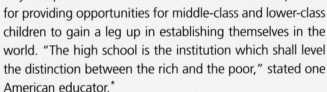 for providing opportunities for middle-class and lower-class children to gain a leg up in establishing themselves in the world. "The high school is the institution which shall level the distinction between the rich and the poor," stated one American educator.*

finished products for the market and building materials needed for bridges, houses, buildings, ships, and roads. Vast stretches of the Great Plains were still underpopulated and

Changes were also taking place at the college level during these years. In the early 1860s, the Republican-controlled Congress passed the Morrill Act, which set aside large tracts of federally owned land and handed them over to the states for the building of colleges that emphasized education in the agricultural and mechanical arts. By 1900, nearly 1,000 such colleges had been established (they were often referred to as "land-grant colleges") with a total enrollment of nearly a quarter-million students!

Higher education was considered important to America's future. Some saw colleges and universities, as well as the other emphases on education, as the answer to America's existing and future problems. Steel magnate Andrew Carnegie wrote about this sentiment in his book *Triumphant Democracy*, published in 1886: "Just see, wherever we peer into the first tiny springs of the national life, how this true panacea for all the ills of the body politic bubbles forth—education, education, education."[**]

This new emphasis on college education also led to the establishment of several colleges by some of the nation's wealthiest tycoons. (Despite the emphasis, only 1 in 400 Americans had a college degree by 1900.) That year, Scottish-American steel baron Andrew Carnegie doled out $2 million to establish the Carnegie Institute of Technology in Pittsburgh, home to his steel empire. Other philanthropists who ponied up money for institutions of higher learning were California railroad builder Leland Stanford; Johns Hopkins, a Baltimore banker; and the founder of Western Union, Ezra Cornell.

---

[*] Time-Life Books, *Prelude to the Century* (Alexandria, Va.: Time-Life Books, 1998), 112.

[**] Ibid.

excessively remote. Cowboys still worked the ranches and drove cattle from Texas to Nebraska, Kansas, and Colorado. Farmers settled on the plains, lured West by the Homestead

Act, which promised free land on the American prairies. Between 1870 and 1900, American settlers, including some new immigrants from Europe, established themselves in the West on 430 million acres of untamed lands, helping to bring the western frontier to a close by the 1890s.

Distance was still the enemy between points of civilization on the American landscape, but the railroads were reducing space by conquering time. Railroads were becoming "industry's best customers."[11] Between 1870 and 1900, railroad companies used 60 percent of the country's steel, as rail line mileage increased four times over; nearly 200,000 miles of track were laid by the beginning of the new century. By 1900, two of every five miles of rail line on Earth crisscrossed the United States. The nation's first transcontinental line was completed in the spring of 1869, and three more were added by 1883. Crossing the 3,000 miles from the Atlantic to the Pacific, a distance that required months of travel just a generation earlier, was reduced to a mere week.

The last three decades of the nineteenth century would signal the beginning of the machine age. Its origins were rooted in the Industrial Revolution, which came to North America from England nearly a century earlier. Waterpower, long harnessed, was outstripped by the power of the steam engine in the years before the Civil War. Before the War of 1812, steam-powered boats were plying American waters from New York to New Orleans, and early factories, with their tall smokestacks, were dotting the landscape of the Northeast. The first American-built railroad locomotive was constructed in 1830. Charles Goodyear first vulcanized rubber in 1839 and, in 1846, Norbert Rillieux revolutionized food production by creating a vacuum evaporator, making canned foods possible and practical. American tinkerers and mechanics were busy inventing the cotton gin, assembly lines, textile mills, repeating revolvers, the passenger elevator, sewing machines, mechanical reaping machines, and steel plows. At the celebration of the nation's centennial (1876) in Philadelphia, visitors gawked at a 1,500-horsepower steam engine on display in Machinery Hall. Nothing else like it existed in the world. The centennial displays included other equally amazing inventions, including the typewriter at which visitors could pay 50¢ to have an expert typist pound out a letter that they could send home to friends or relatives. Perhaps more important than any other mechanical gadget at the exposition was the one patented the previous year (Patent Number 174,465) by Alexander Graham Bell: the telephone. Over the next generation, a million of Bell's communication devices were in use in America. As writer Fon Boardman, Jr., summed it up, "The United States was on its way to being the talkingest nation in the world."[12]

Other electronic wonders would be invented during this age. While widespread use of the telegraph began in the 1840s, Western Union, the largest telegraph company in the country, hired one of the nation's most prolific inventors, Thomas Alva Edison, to take Bell's device and apply it to a large-scale transmission system. In the process of working on that project in 1877, Edison inadvertently invented the phonograph, which reproduced the human voice for the first time in history. Edison would make other equally important contributions to the new "modern" age of the late nineteenth century; he received more than 1,000 patents in his lifetime. Working out of his laboratory in New Jersey in 1879, he perfected the first practical incandescent lightbulb. Within three years, he brought a power station online on the lower end of Manhattan to generate the electricity needed to begin lighting New York City. By 1900, 20 million electric lights were changing night

During the last three decades of the nineteenth century, electronic inventions such as the telephone, phonograph, and lightbulb were just some of the wonders that captured the imagination of Americans. Here, Thomas Edison poses with his phonograph, which played back recorded sound.

into day. Edison had several other successes, including a motion picture camera and a projector.

Americans entered the rank and file of the age of industrialization, becoming factory workers and miners by the thousands. They were part of a great social shift in the United States that added millions of new residents to the ever-growing numbers that lived in the big cities from New York to

Chicago, St. Louis to Cincinnati. This new industrialization placed the United States at the top of important industries. The United States was, by the end of the century, producing more than 30 percent of the world's coal, 34 percent of its iron, and nearly 37 percent of its steel.

While the changes were extraordinary, it was the pace of change that drew the attention and concern of many Americans, and those "changes were not only in size but in kind."[13] The America of 1900 found fewer than 40 percent of Americans working in agriculture and an equal number living in cities. The cities were filling, it seemed to some, to capacity. Horace Greeley, the editor of an influential New York City newspaper, noted the shift even by the late 1860s. "We cannot all live in cities," he warned, "yet nearly all seem determined to do so."[14] As early as 1870, approximately a dozen American cities boasted at least 100,000 residents each. The numbers were staggering. Between 1870 and 1900, Detroit grew from 80,000 to 285,000, and Atlanta increased from 22,000 to 90,000. Philadelphia, nearly two centuries old by then, nearly doubled in population, from 675,000 to 1.3 million. Out on the prairies of Illinois, Chicago reached the 1.7 million mark after struggling back from a devastating fire that had destroyed much of the city in 1871. Frontier Los Angeles, out in the distance reaches of southern California, had been home to only 5,700 in 1870. By 1900, its population had ballooned to more than 100,000. Ahead of them all was New York City, whose population reached 3.4 million by 1900, after its five boroughs were consolidated in 1898.

These new city dwellers came from the four corners of the globe, many from eastern and southern Europe— Poles, Czechs, Italians, Romanians, Greeks, Hungarians, and Russian Jews. They reached American shores by the millions during the final decades of the 1800s. Just in the 1880s alone, 5 million foreigners immigrated to American shores, lured by stories of streets paved with gold and freedom for all.

However, the majority of the new city residents were already U.S. citizens. They were Americans who left the rural farms in droves to seek their fortunes and livelihoods in the cities. A portion of these displaced farm folk were driven from the rural country by the new farm machinery, some of which could do the work of a half-dozen farmhands. Others were simply young men and women, some veterans of the Civil War, ready to leave the simplicity and, sometimes, the aching boredom of fields and furrows, to pursue urban dreams.

SKYSCRAPERS AND ELECTRICITY

These American urban landscapes presented "a façade as filled with magic as had been the dreams of the immigrants."[15] Skyscrapers towered higher than any European cathedral towers, their stone exteriors gleaming with the spit and polish of a new American era. In 1884, the city of Chicago became home to a 10-story building, the Home Insurance Building, its framework formed by a steel skeleton. Just eight years later, after similar skyscrapers were built in New York, St. Louis, and Buffalo, the Chicago skyline was interrupted by a 22-story construction, the Masonic Temple, then the tallest building in the United States. It would be surpassed, of course, by the turn of the century with the completion of the Ivins Syndicate Building on Park Row in New York City, a 29-story edifice that towered 382 feet above Manhattan Island.

The interiors of such buildings were as impressive as their newly designed exteriors, with the interconnected twin miracles of running water and indoor bathrooms. Electricity was an old power newly harnessed in these cities. Humming

In 1892, Chicago's 302-foot- (192-meter-) high Masonic Temple became the tallest building in the United States (in terms of highest occupied story). Located at the corner of Randolph and State streets, the building remained Chicago's tallest building until new zoning laws permitted the construction of skyscrapers in the 1920s.

electric elevators whisked visitors, businessmen, and tenants up 20 floors or more. All along the city streets, a spider's web of electrical lines ran from pole to pole, carrying power from generators to buildings and lighting up the urban world. At night, the cities gleamed with street lamps and remained lively long after the sun went down. In Boston, at the Bijou Theatre, evening performances were possible thanks to the introduction of an electric light system that included 650 lightbulbs. In New York, at the tricorner of Fifth Avenue, Broadway, and 23rd Street (where the future Flatiron Building would stand), those on the street could marvel at a 50-foot-tall sign that featured a huge pickle lit up by green lights, along with rows of white bulbs that spelled "HEINZ, 57 Varieties." Such wonders were hallmarks of the approaching century. The inroads made by electricity were, however, made slowly. As late as 1899, only 5 percent of the machines operating in American factories were powered by electricity. Within another 20 years, however, 55 percent of factory machines were electric.

Electricity moved people, as well. On America's late-nineteenth-century thoroughfares, electric "horseless" trolleys seemed to fly by constantly, at the speed of 20 miles an hour. By 1890, more than 200 cities across the country had installed electric trolleys. (Out in San Francisco, a city by the bay built on rolling, steep hills, a cable-car system was introduced in 1873.) By 1900, there were 30,000 trolley cars in use in the United States, rolling along on 15,000 miles of track. By then, Boston already had an electric-powered subway system, and New York would begin construction on its first system in 1900. The city had already built the nation's first elevated railroad in 1878, "a steam-driven, noisy, and a ghastly fire hazard, but it was worshiped as progress and imitated."[16] The cities were redefining America. As one British writer, Sir John Leng, wrote of one American metropolis, "The thoroughfares are crowded, busy and bustling; and abounding signs of life and energy in the people are everywhere apparent."[17]

BUILDING A FUTURE FROM STEEL

This new urban world of America was built from old material reinvented for the late nineteenth century—steel. On July 4, 1874, just two years shy of the young nation's hundredth birthday, the first significant steel structure in the United States—the Eads Bridge of St. Louis—was officially opened. It stretched 1,500 feet across the Mississippi River, and with its opening, the age of American steel began to take shape. Less than a decade earlier, the Civil War had brought steel into the forefront, as factories produced metal items from cannons to telegraph wire.

The invention of steel brought an end to another era of metal, the Iron Age. Steel was, after all, no more than iron with its carbon impurities burned off, which gave the metal greater strength and durability—but the difference was as extraordinary as night and day. Earlier buildings had been limited in height and size because of "the brittle quality and weight of iron and masonry."[18] The new innovation of converting iron to steel, called the Bessemer process, made the production of steel not only inexpensive but practical in large quantities through mass production. Eads Bridge proved this clearly. Just two days before the bridge's inauguration, Eads put its steel framework to the test by ordering 14 railroad locomotives, weighing a total of 700 tons, onto the bridge. Soon, the nation embraced steel. In less than 10 years, another great steel span, the Brooklyn Bridge, was built. It was the first suspension bridge supported by steel cables, and it connected Brooklyn with Manhattan Island. Its builder, John Augustus Roebling, was a veteran of the Civil War. Steel would recast the country; it even made its mark in the remote wildernesses of the West in the form of barbed wire and railroad lines.

The first suspension bridge supported by steel cables in the United States, the Brooklyn Bridge spans the East River and connects the New York City boroughs of Brooklyn and Manhattan. Opened for traffic in 1883, the suspension bridge was once the longest of its kind in the world.

CHANGES IN RETAIL

The new urban world, filled with upwardly mobile people, also created great marketplaces in which the vast array of manufactured goods could be sold. The items available were endless—factory-made shoes, clothing, furniture, books, even foods such as canned meats. Such goods could be produced cheaply, many for the first time in history, and were available for the masses. They could be purchased in small neighborhood stores, just as they had been throughout the 1800s and even earlier, but the new cities boasted new marketplaces. Retail stores included new innovations, such as department stores, chain stores, and even shopping malls. One of the first of these malls opened in Cleveland in 1890. Two facing fronts and four stories of shops and offices stretched longer than a football field, inviting customers to shop under a great canopy of glass and steel. Wrought-iron railings flanked an open promenade, ushering in a new age of merchandizing everything from cigars to women's notions, all under one protective roof.

One of the earliest department stores in the United States was opened by one of Chicago's great entrepreneurs, Marshall Field. Having built his commercial success on a simple dry-goods store, Field would convert his retail power into a department store with annual sales that reached $35 million by 1890. There were other retail innovators, as well, such as Frank W. Woolworth, a dry-goods clerk who one day in 1874 placed a pile of items on a tray, pricing them at 5 and 10 cents each. Women shoppers snatched up the entire inventory before the end of the business day. Inspired, Woolworth would soon open his own store in Lancaster, Pennsylvania, as Woolworth's Five- and Ten-Cent Store. By 1880, he owned 25 such stores, each producing annual sales of one million dollars. The mass retail market had reached the hands and pocketbooks of American shoppers. An English visitor shopping along New York City's 14th Street marveled at the abundance and affordability of the new American marketplace: "It is a perfect bazaar. Not only is there a brilliant display in the windows of everything from Paris-imported bonnets to pink-satin boots, but the sidewalk is fringed with open-air stalls, heaped high with pretty things, many of them absurdly cheap."[19]

A BRIGHT FUTURE?

Americans entered the new century with great expectations. Without knowing it, the nation was living between two great wars—the Civil War and World War I. The country refused to look back and instead had an eye toward the future. For so many, what might happen next in American history held a good deal of excitement and optimism. As the new century opened, the January 1 issue of the *New York Times* included this optimistic observation about America's future: "The year 1899 was a year of wonders. . . . It would be easy to speak of the twelve months just passed as the banner year were we not already confident that the distinction of highest records must presently pass to the year 1900. . . . The outlook on the threshold of the new year is extremely bright."[20]

The new year, however, would find many Americans dissatisfied with the "modern" world that had been created during the decades that led to the twentieth century. Much had taken place that might be considered improvements in the American way of life, but there were problems, too— big problems. Those same elements that had re-created America in positive ways—mechanization, industrialization, urbanization, commercialization—had also delivered misery, injustice, and class struggle to the United States on a scale never before seen. Those were the problems that Progressives of the early twentieth century would take on as their challenge.

3

How the Other Half Lives

As America steered toward the close of the nineteenth century, many aspects of life in the United States appeared bright and hopeful. Millions of Europeans were attracted to America and established their new homes in the young republic because of such opportunities. However, life was not hopeful, bright, or enviable for many Americans at the end of the 1800s. Despite its many positive attributes, the United States was facing serious problems, some of them as old as the country itself and others much more recent in origin. The Progressive movement of the early twentieth century began largely because a group of Americans recognized the existence of these problems and believed that they could help bring about changes that would either eliminate them or lessen their extent. The challenges they faced would be enormous.

FROM AGRICULTURAL TO URBAN

In 1870, the vast majority of Americans had lived on farms, just as their families had for generations. Many such families were self-sufficient, growing their own food, teaching their own children to read and write, working to make a home for themselves, making many of the everyday items that they needed, and often getting along without the things they did not perceive as needs. With the approach of the twentieth century, much of that changed for many Americans. In the years after the Civil War, the United States was becoming more industrialized as factories were built near major cities. As workers flocked to the cities, the country became more urbanized. Many Americans stopped working for themselves and became employees of large companies and giant corporations, which often treated them impersonally. Those who did not work in great mills and factories typically found jobs as domestic servants, seamstresses, unskilled laborers, and day laborers. Such workers were paid wages for their labor, which they used to pay rent and buy food and other necessary items. Removed from the land and locked into city life, a larger percentage of Americans, including the new immigrant population, had to buy what they needed to survive, drawing them into a market economy. This was a world over which few Americans had any real control.

For many, the pay was low, creating a vast amount of poverty in the United States. The average workweek consisted of 55 to 60 hours—10-hour days 5 days a week and half a workday on Saturday. Some jobs, such as those in the steel industry, required an 84-hour work schedule—12-hour days 7 days a week. Despite all of this labor, the average unskilled American worker received $10 a week in wages. Those who worked in the textile mills might be paid 75¢ for 10 hours of labor. In garment factories, female "pressers" might make an equivalent wage of 8¢ an hour. In the last decades of the nineteenth century, many industries worked at full capacity only during a portion of the year and then closed down for a season, leaving their workers without jobs and without income for several months.

In 1904, writer Robert Hunter published a study entitled *Poverty*, in which he estimated that "at least 10 million of

America's 76 million people were so poor they could not 'obtain those necessaries which will permit them to maintain a state of physical efficiency.'"[21] A second study published two years later by an American economist concluded that three of every five adult male workers in the United States did not earn enough money to support a family. By that figure, 50 million Americans could be classified as poor. By the turn of the century, millions of wage earners in America were living below a "standard that a man would demand for his horses or slaves."[22]

In many ways, the injustices of the American labor system of the late nineteenth century applied to workers whether they were skilled or unskilled. The new technologies and machines of the ever-modernizing era were even replacing skilled laborers just as quickly as the unskilled. American business was just that—business. The pressures of the marketplace called for goods to be produced as cheaply as possible, and factory managers did not want to deal with skilled workers who might "overvalue" their abilities. Control of production fell increasingly out of the workers' hands and into those of the owners, investors, and capitalists.

POOR WORKING CONDITIONS

There were some reasonably bright spots in the new labor market of the late 1800s. Women had more opportunities to work outside the home and went into classrooms, storefronts, and offices as teachers, floor clerks, secretaries, and stenographers in droves. By 1880, 8,000 women worked as sales clerks. A decade later, their numbers had jumped to nearly 60,000. The women who held these jobs were usually white and native born, whereas immigrant and black women worked as domestic servants and in sweatshops as underpaid textile workers. Women who worked in sweatshops might receive no more than $200 a year for their work. Women

Female immigrants from eastern and southern Europe were often forced to work in textile factories at rates as low as $200 a year. Here, immigrant workers toil in a sweatshop located in New York City's garment district.

had jobs, yes, but the salaries for such work were usually extremely low. It is true that the "real wages for workers increased as the prices of farm products and manufactured goods fell during the deflation that lasted until the late 1890s,"[23] but the hours were still long and working conditions less than attractive.

Workers sometimes labored under conditions that would be considered appalling by today's standards. Mill workers struggled at their jobs in loud noise, extreme heat, and danger. Those who worked in mines and factories or on the nation's railroads faced equal hazards. Accidents were common: 35,000 workers were killed between 1880 and 1900, and another half-million were seriously injured.

Such accidents did not result in compensation for workers. There were almost no legal protections provided by the states or the federal government. An injured worker received no compensation, and families of killed workers received no death benefits. Workers could be dismissed at any time for no reason, and when the economy had a downturn, workers could expect to lose their jobs. Laborers did not receive health benefits or pensions. The system even abused children. During the last decades of the nineteenth century, nearly 200,000 children under the age of 16 labored in American factories and mills "with no health and safety restrictions to protect them."[24]

EFFORTS TO ORGANIZE WORKERS

Workers who struggled under such poor conditions sometimes tried to find ways to fight the system. They might try to challenge this new, lopsided system of work and management, but there was little they could do to fight it. Labor tried to organize itself, but the law usually worked against it. At the center of the relationship between employer and worker was a concept known as the "iron law of wages." This idea was based on the assumption that employers were free to find workers who would accept the lowest pay possible, driving out of the market anyone who demanded higher pay. If one worker would not accept a given set of wages for a specific amount of work, there was generally someone else who would. Workers had to accept what they were offered. When the Pennsylvania-based Amalgamated Association of Iron and Steel Workers went out on strike demanding higher wages, the steel mill owners ignored them. After five months on the picket lines, the workers had no choice but to return to work.

These last decades of the nineteenth century saw a surge in labor organizations, however. Few labor unions existed in

THE RAILROADS

Just as urban dwellers were caught up in a world of bribes, political payoffs, and citywide corruption, rural farmers found themselves victims of another system. During the 1870s and 1880s, farmers fanned out across the West, planting themselves and their families in remote corners of the country. As they established their farms, they became dependent on the ever-advancing reach of the country's railroads. All farmers longed to have a rail line built as close to their small towns or farmlands as possible. Railroads were the means of getting farm produce to market, and the farmer stuck far off a rail line might have difficulty making a profit from his agricultural endeavors.

The railroads became a double-edged sword. Because railroads usually had no regional rivals, farmers were often at their mercy, forced to pay whatever freight rates the railroads charged. One of the great problems for farmers after the Civil War, which provided great markets for American produce, was a crisis in productivity. As more and more farmers, using newer technology and farming innovations, became more productive, the price or value of their farm commodities declined. Farmers were simply overproductive. A bushel of wheat sold for $1.20 in 1881 but had sold for twice that amount 10 or 15 years earlier. By 1889, a bushel of wheat sold for only 70¢. In 1881, cotton sold for 11¢ a pound, but, by 1890, the price had dropped to 8.5 cents per pound. Growing a crop was hardly paying for itself.

Add to the equation the railroads and their high freight rates. Rates were often higher for farmers than for anyone else who used the rail systems to haul goods. Because they were generally unregulated by the government, railroads were able to charge farmers (as small haulers) a higher freight rate per ton per mile than they charged a large hauler, such as a stockyard, grain elevator, or warehouse company. Railroads were not the cause of the serious drop in prices that took place during the 1880s, but their treatment of farmers only generated anger and bitterness. In time, farmers and ranchers across the Far West, Midwest, and South would band together—socially, economically, and politically—to fight the railroads and their unethical practices.

the United States prior to the Civil War, but they sprang up quickly after it. One of the first was the National Labor Union (NLU), a collection of trade unions that was established a year after the war had ended. Its members campaigned on behalf of an eight-hour workday and better wages, but had little success. The Knights of Labor was organized by the 1870s, gaining more than 40,000 members by 1882. This organization wanted the government to pass laws to protect workers, as well as the eight-hour workday. It was an open group that accepted workers as diverse as skilled artisans, Southern farmers, and women. Its membership numbers peaked around 100,000 by the mid-1880s. Labor strife and alleged union-inspired violence blamed on the Knights of Labor in 1886 caused the group to decline. Another important union, the American Federation of Labor, would gain 150,000 members by the 1880s, as well, and double that number in just a few more years. This organization, too, failed to bring about significant social change.

A SEGREGATED SOUTH

Another problem that some Americans faced during the latter decades of the 1800s was based on racism and segregation. The Civil War had brought about an end to legal slavery in the United States, but the millions of blacks who were freed from slavery often found their lives just as difficult after they gained their freedom. Racial prejudice was everywhere and was commonly accepted among white Americans of all classes. The federal government did make some attempts to prohibit racial discrimination after the war through legislation such as the Civil Rights acts of 1866 and 1875. The latter act prohibited racial discrimination in public accommodations. In 1883, the U.S. Supreme Court decided against the 1875 act, ruling that the Fourteenth Amendment to the Constitution, created just after the Civil War to provide equal rights to blacks, only restricted governmental discrimination, not that from private businesses or citizens. A new era of racism spread across the American South and beyond, as blacks were barred from restaurants, hotels, and inns; public means of transportation; and other public places. Segregation was, once again, an acceptable way to treat blacks.

Black rights were continually disregarded in the United States during these decades. Federal laws, including the Fifteenth Amendment, provided guarantees for black voters, but those laws were sometimes subverted by state and local laws that required blacks to pay taxes or to pass a literacy test before voting. Whites were routinely allowed to vote without satisfying these same restrictions.

Blacks were also mistreated in the workforce, especially in the South. As former slaves, they were often illiterate and poor and had few skills other than farming. They were prime targets for mistreatment in the decades after the Civil War because they were still living in the South amid the next generation of white Southerners. Cheap labor was as much the rule among Southerners as with Northern factory owners. Blacks worked in a new way as farm laborers for white landowners. Some became tenant farmers, "renting" the land and providing the tools necessary to farm and produce a crop, including seeds, plows, and mules. Come harvest time, tenant farmers were allowed to sell their crops and paid the landowner in cash or with a percentage of their crops. Other blacks (and some poor whites, as well) worked as sharecroppers. They were the poorest farm workers, bringing nothing to the equation other than their labor. The white landowners provided everything needed to raise a crop. These materials were given to the black sharecropper "on credit." When the crops were brought in and sold, sharecroppers made very little because they needed to use nearly all of their profits to pay off their debts to the landowners. If one year's crop was poor, the sharecropper might not make enough even to get out of debt. The result was an endless cycle of abuse and near slavery. Southern laws provided no protection to such victims of poverty and racism.

PERILS OF URBAN LIVING

Rural living had its challenges, injustices, and hard edges, but life in the new American cities of the 1880s and 1890s posed special difficulties of its own. After 1880, U.S. cities grew at an astonishing rate, too fast for city officials to make the appropriate changes in order to accommodate such large numbers of people crammed into the urban jungle. There was simply not enough living space or decent housing for the teeming masses that were flocking in from the rural areas and arriving daily by the hundreds onboard ocean-going steamers from foreign countries. Even for middle- and upper-class urbanites, the single-family dwelling was nearly nonexistent. Apartment living became the norm. Poorer residents of the cities were stuffed into tenement housing, apartment buildings that rose six or seven stories tall with brick edifices that masked the horrors of living in the worst neighborhoods. During the decades after the Civil War, New York City became home to approximately 20,000 such buildings, "most of them 25 feet wide and 100 feet deep."[25] These tenements provided no luxuries and barely offered even the basics of decent living. They were poorly heated in the winter, reeking hot in the summer, and dark, with nearly no windows.

By the late 1870s, with the passage of a few laws that required at least some ventilation, the new design was the "dumbbell tenement." These featured small, indented

In response to the influx of immigrants to New York City after the Civil War, the city built tenements to house these newcomers who could not afford to live in traditional apartment buildings. Here, an Italian family huddles together in one of New York's cramped tenement rooms.

windows along the buildings' side walls. Such buildings looked more attractive on the exterior, but they were still crammed with dozens of people per floor, each living in tiny, nearly unlit rooms. As writer William Dean Howells observed, "To be in it, and not have the distance, is to inhale the stenches of the neglected street and to catch the yet fouler and dreadfuller poverty-smell which breathes from the open doorways."[26]

In addition to the restrictions posed by living in poorly designed tenement houses, the poor urban dwellers of the late nineteenth century faced other problems, including those found on the streets below. There, the foul odor of manure was constant and garbage might fill the alleys. Sewers were poor and, in some places, nonexistent. Factory towns were noted for the poor air quality, as factory smokestacks belched plumes of dark, sooty air, sometimes thick with sulfur and other chemicals. Urban water supplies were often poor: In Philadelphia, the water supply was "not only distasteful and unwholesome for drinking, but offensive for bathing purposes."[27] Conditions were sometimes described best by those who only visited the tenements, such as an Italian actor who paid a call to a fellow countryman's neighborhood: "It is impossible to describe the mud, the dirt, the filth, the stinking humidity, the nuisances, the disorder of the streets."[28] When city architects in Boston reported on the condition of that city's slums, they told of "dirty and battered walls and ceilings, dark cellars with water standing in them, alleys littered with garbage and filth, broken and leaking drain-pipes . . . dark and filthy water-closets, closets long frozen or otherwise out of order . . . houses so dilapidated and so much settled that they are dangerous."[29]

Other problems that plagued city dwellers in the poor districts included high crime, high unemployment, spousal and child abuse, alcoholism, and prostitution. Many of these poor victims were recent immigrants who had arrived in the United States with few marketable skills, no command of the English language, and customs and folkways that made them curiosities at best and despised by native-born Americans at worst. Poles, Czechs, Russians, Italians, and others were all living under the most difficult of circumstances. In New York, the tenements were filled to capacity. One of the worst was the Tenth Ward, a Jewish community where, by 1900, residents lived so close together that their numbers were equivalent to 900 people per acre, making their neighborhood one of the most crowded in the world.

POLITICS OF THE MACHINE

These same American cities that were becoming crowded and dirty had limited municipal services. These wards were often administered by groups of politicians who sought public office for personal gain. Because these council members were voted in by districts, they often traded votes, exchanged political favors with one another, and stood in the way of any legislative decisions that might harm their voters in some way. To give mayors more power, politicians sometimes created structures called "political machines."

The "machine" oversaw a citywide organization "that dominated city politics [and] consisted of an interlocking system of operations in each ward that delivered votes for their party at city and county conventions."[30] Politicians relied on the "machine" to guarantee votes on each election day, resulting in the reelection of the parties in power. Those who were out drumming up votes were typically referred to as "ward bosses," men who got people to vote in their given neighborhoods. Such ward bosses were well known to their constituents and helped people get jobs or aided them if they came up on the wrong side of the law. Ward leaders kept constant contact with their ward populations, attending weddings, funerals, and wakes to keep themselves on popular footing. If a family had a fire and lost everything, the ward boss would soon be on its doorstep, offering a new place to live, food, furniture, and comfort. It was understood that such connections and favors were maintained and performed to gain votes on election day. From top to bottom, the political machine was a corrupt system.

Ward bosses were often convinced that they provided a public service to their communities simply by being available, even if political goals were the motivation. As a Boston ward boss expressed, "I think that there's got to be in every ward somebody that any bloke can come to—no matter what he's done—and get help. Help, you understand, none of your law and justice, but help!"[31]

At the top of the political machine food chain was the city boss, who remained in power as long as the ward leaders turned out the voters on his behalf. The bosses then rewarded the wards that supported them by providing their residents with job opportunities. Some of the more famous political machine bosses of the era were Boston's mayor, John F. "Honey Fitz" Fitzgerald, grandfather of future U.S. president John F. Kennedy, Jr., and William Magear Tweed, who ran the infamous "Tweed Ring" in New York City beginning in the early 1860s. The bosses also controlled all city contracts, giving them to friends and supporters and sometimes costing the cities great amounts of money because of the high level of corruption, payoffs, and bribes that were part of the process. Many municipal construction projects, including building streets, subways, and sewers; laying gas lines; and erecting elevated train platforms, were opportunities for graft and corruption on the part of the city bosses. Through it all, the city bosses lined their pockets. American city government at the turn of the century was more often than not corrupt. There were those who spoke out against such corruption. A president of Cornell University laid down the damning charge that America's cities were "the most corrupt in Christendom."[32]

4

Fighting Back with Politics

The picture of the last three decades of the nineteenth century emerges more clearly when the good and the bad are placed side by side. The era could claim great surges of success, inventiveness, and positive social change. It could also hang its head in shame for the injustices that were placed on the shoulders of its working class, its newly arrived immigrants, its urban dwellers, its minorities, and its women and children. The era would not end before several groups of Americans took serious steps to challenge the world in which they struggled. One of those groups would be America's farmers. They were accustomed to difficult times—they were, after all, stewards of the soil and familiar with all the problems that went along with farming in the nineteenth century—but they had finally had enough by the late 1880s and early 1890s. They were not happy with railroads or the government, and they would take steps against both.

Their earliest efforts were in the 1860s and 1870s, when farmers banded together in a way similar to organized labor. In 1867, a Bureau of Agriculture clerk named Oliver H. Kelley organized the National Grange of the Order of the Patrons of Husbandry (called "The Grange"). Within eight years, the organization claimed 800,000 members and 20,000 local chapters, called *Granges*, an ancient Latin term that means "granary." It was a cooperative of sorts, designed to pool farm resources to build grain elevators, warehouses, and farm implement factories. This would allow the farmers to purchase items that they needed in order to farm at wholesale prices and to bypass the greedy storage facility operators who gouged them with high storage fees. They even set up their own mail-order catalog business before the days of Montgomery Ward or Sears and Roebuck.

The organization had limited success, and members were often frustrated that it did not have much political power. In 1880, another organization was established to address that issue. The purpose of the National Farmers' Alliance (NFAs) was to "seek more favorable railroad and tax legislation and to legalize Grange insurance companies."[33] Within two years, the NFA had 100,000 members and, as economic times became worse by the early 1890s, new members were joining at the rate of 1,000 per week. The key to the organization was at the grassroots level. Local chapters of the alliance put pressure on state legislatures to pass laws to restrict the harmful activities of railroads and to regulate large business corporations. Members called for the government to establish "agricultural sub treasuries," government-owned warehouses and grain elevators where agriculturalists could store their produce until the market for a given commodity improved. In the meantime, with their produce safely and cheaply stored away for a better day, farmers hoped to receive government-supported loans worth 80 percent of the value of their corn, wheat, or other produce.

A THIRD PARTY FOR FARMERS

Ultimately, the National Farmers' Alliance did not succeed in helping many farmers economically; however, it was from this organization, as well as other farm groups and their various political causes, that the farm movement finally formed a political party of its own. The organization expanded dramatically between 1886 and 1890, bringing farmers together to listen to speeches, enjoy times together, and support one another. By 1889, an organized national effort on the part of the NFA brought great membership gains in the Dakotas, Nebraska, and especially Kansas. That year, farmers took the next natural step in organizing. In December 1889, representatives of the farming interests gathered in St. Louis to plan their next step. From those discussions, the delegates organized themselves for the national off-year elections scheduled for the next year.

During the election campaigns of 1890, the farm protest movement again made itself heard, mostly through speeches that gave support to one candidate or another. Some spoke in favor of a third political party, one established by the farming interests across the country, but this idea was postponed until February 1892. Throughout the previous two years, the farmers had waited to see what types of proagricultural legislation might be passed by the various farm-state legislatures. There would be little progress on behalf of farmers, though, and both the Republican and Democratic parties (especially the Democrats) fought to derail NFA ideas.

Frustrated, farmers began to organize a third political party, known as the People's Party, or, as derived from Latin, the Populists. They held their first national convention in Omaha, Nebraska, on the Fourth of July in 1892. During the convention, Populist delegates worked hard to determine their party's platform for the presidential campaign that would take place in the fall. On July 4, the platform was officially adopted. The measures the Populists supported called for a wide range of political reforms and supports for the nation's farmers. Planks in the platform included 1) an increase in the nation's money supply through a dramatic increase in silver currency; 2) government ownership of the nation's railroads, telegraphs, and telephones; 3) the return to the government of all formerly federal lands held by the railroads, as well as other corporations, in excess of their needs; 4) the implementation of a graduated income tax that required those with higher incomes to pay higher rates of tax; 5) a system of government-owned warehouses and grain elevators in which farm products could be stored cheaply until the prices on farm commodities improved; and 6) the passage of political reforms, including the adoption of the direct election of United States senators, as well as the secret ballot, the initiative, and the referendum.

At this convention, a potential candidate came to the front. He was a North Carolinian named Leonidas L. Polk. A lifelong farmer, he was also the editor of the *Progressive Farmer* magazine and was an important advocate of farming interests across the South. Polk had gone to college to become a lawyer, and had fought in the Civil War, gaining the rank of brigadier general. After the war, he had made attempts to enter politics but was considered too conservative for the Republican Party because of his strict morality and support of Prohibition. He finally joined a third party, the Greenback Party, in the late 1870s, and won a seat in Congress. He ran and lost as their presidential candidate two years later but served two additional congressional terms as a Greenback supporter.

Polk unexpectedly died within a month of the Omaha convention, however, and in his place, the convention delegates chose James B. Weaver as the Populist Party candidate. When the National Farmers' Alliance was formed, Weaver had joined and became a champion of the organization. (The Populist Party was, in some ways, the successor to the Greenback Party, because many of the Greenback Party's members had been farmers.)

During the 1892 election, Weaver received more than one million popular votes and won 22 electoral votes. Weaver's numbers at the polls that year represented the efforts of a poor third-party showing, however. It was obvious that the Populists would not gain the presidency without help from one or the other of the two political parties. By 1896, a coalition was formed that banded the Populists and the Democrats together in something of a common cause. Both parties nominated the same candidate—a Nebraska congressman named William Jennings Bryan.

Between the two presidential election years, the nation had suffered through a severe depression, one of the worst in American history. Not only had farmers been negatively affected, many other groups of Americans, especially underpaid laborers, such as factory workers, had felt its impact as well. The Depression of 1893 had not translated into great gains for the Populists. In the 1894 congressional elections, "the Populists were almost as disappointed as the Democrats with the outcome."[34] The number of Populists in Congress dropped from 11 to 7, and the poor economy continued through the term of President Grover Cleveland, the Democrat who had been elected in 1892.

This depression would set the stage for the 1896 election. The Populists hoped the poor economy would help them elect William Jennings Bryan, their standard bearer from Nebraska, to the White House. However, a conservative element across the nation was put off by the Populist call for an increase in the money supply by having the federal government print more paper money and mint more silver coins (silver had dramatically lost its value during the 1880s and '90s), and turned instead to the Republican candidate, William McKinley of Ohio.

In 1896, both the Democratic and Populist parties nominated U.S. congressman William Jennings Bryan of Nebraska for president. Although Bryan (*above*) was defeated by Republican William McKinley, many historians consider the election to be the hardest fought in U.S. history.

In 1897, the newly inaugurated McKinley and the nation's other conservative Republicans appeared to have a clear road before them. The depression that had plagued the nation and Democratic president Grover Cleveland from 1893 through 1896 had vanished and given way to a general prosperity. Even farmers, who had struggled for decades with poor farm prices, were better off. The European wheat crop was down by 30 percent, providing a larger market for American wheat and other grains and allowing American farmers to export 150 million bushels. (The American crop that year was gigantic.) Republicans controlled not only the White House, but Congress as well. The party passed the Dingley Tariff that year, a business-friendly move that raised average tariff rates to a new high of 57 percent. With so much prosperity affecting many Americans of every economic class, it was easy for many in the late 1890s to put aside the demands of the Populists, who soon died out as a party, as well as other reform-minded groups.

EARLY ATTEMPTS AT REFORM

During the Cleveland years, the United States witnessed several reform movements that paralleled the Populists' call for change across the country. Some of the important motivators and backers for these reforms were various Christian religious groups that sought goals such as controls on the sale and use of alcoholic beverages. Leading the way on behalf of this national cause was the Woman's Christian Temperance Union (WCTU), which campaigned through local chapters in many American cities, towns, and rural villages. There were also reform calls on behalf of women's rights and urban political reform. The Depression of 1893 only managed to make life in the cities worse for many urbanites, and the call for city government reform seemed to be everywhere. By the mid-1890s, organizations such as the National Municipal League were established (1894), and the First National Conference for Good City Government was held. These efforts were among the early calls for city reform that would one day be an important leg of the Progressive reform agenda.

Some of the voices that spoke on behalf of these early 1890s reform calls were heard. In Wisconsin, a Republican politician named Robert M. La Follette began to organize political backing for reform by attacking urban problems such as corruption and political machines, which he believed were direct challenges to American democracy. La Follette, "a small wiry man with a big head made even bigger by a bush of hair,"[35] had opened his political career with limited success as a Republican politician. A lawyer by training, La Follette had first served as a Wisconsin district attorney, which he followed up with three congressional terms that ended in defeat in 1890.

LA FOLLETTE'S PROGRESSIVE AGENDA

A decade later, La Follette would return to the political trail and was elected as a Progressive Republican governor with a majority of more than 100,000 state votes. Even as he entered the state's top political office, La Follette intended to create a greater level of public control over his state's government. Among the reforms that the Wisconsin politician called for were primary elections, through which candidates for office could be selected by the voters rather than by political bosses and professional politicians, who met behind closed doors. He also advocated the political reform known as the initiative, which allowed the citizens of a state the power to propose their own legislation through a petition process, thus bypassing state legislators who might not favor the proposed acts. La Follette also supported another political reform, the referendum, which would allow an existing law to be placed directly to a vote of the people. They could either accept or reject it, thus eliminating laws the public did not like or support.

These political reforms were all important to La Follette, but he was just as interested in using state government to curb the power of big businesses. He thought it was important that competition exist in the business arena, which

LA FOLLETTE AND PHILETUS SAWYER

Among the names that are most important to the Progressive movement in the United States, one stands almost in a category by itself. He was a small man from Wisconsin, but the work he performed on behalf of the Progressive cause spanned decades. However, this significant personality and contributor to the movement almost lost his political voice before he had an opportunity to make his mark on the movement.

In 1890, Robert La Follette was defeated in Wisconsin's congressional election. He was running for a fourth consecutive term as a Republican representative. A Democratic sweep of his state's elections that year left him out of politics and returning to private law practice. Disappointed, La Follette nevertheless hoped that one day he would be reelected to the House and could take up his Progressive agenda on a national level.

Then, the following year, La Follette had a personal and professional experience that altered his life. He was approached by a Wisconsin senator, Philetus Sawyer, who had made a fortune in the lumber business. In 1891, Sawyer was in control of the Republican Party in his state, and all political decisions of any importance were made through him. Sawyer made La Follette an offer of money, which he tried to pass off as a lawyer fee. Sawyer was concerned about and had an interest in a case that had been assigned to a Wisconsin judge who happened to be La Follette's brother-in-law. La Follette interpreted Sawyer's offer as nothing more than a bribe to get him to intervene

meant that he was highly opposed to big corporations that operated as monopolies, thus keeping competitiveness to a minimum. One of his special targets was the state's railroads. He supported government regulation and other laws to control them and their long arm of economic power.

Even as La Follette supported these political and economic changes, he did not try to push all of them at once immediately after he became Wisconsin's governor. First, he in the case and wield an influence. La Follette rejected the offer of money. Angry, the Wisconsin lawyer informed his brother-in-law of the bribery attempt and reported it to the newspapers, as well.

Embarrassed and angry, Senator Sawyer sought revenge against La Follette and tried to squelch any further political future for the Progressive Republican. La Follette refused to roll over and have his future dreams of political Progressivism dashed, however. He fought against Sawyer, building up a political organization of support separate from Sawyer and the existing Republican Party system in the state. He appealed to supporters in the major cities, including Madison and Milwaukee, and also went after grassroots support from the smaller communities and the farming regions.

He continued to amass his political backing without the help of Sawyer and, by 1900, attended the Republican state convention, seeking the party's nomination for governor. At the convention, the majority of his party's delegates supported him and he gained the nomination. The election that November was a sweet win for La Follette. He garnered 102,000 more votes than his opponents and was elected governor. With this recapture of the state's political imagination, La Follette was able to pursue his dream of Progressive reform, despite all efforts by Senator Sawyer to keep him out of the political ring. As a postscript to this clash of political wills, Senator Sawyer died in 1900 and Robert La Follette was elected to the Senate six years later.

pushed a pair of measures—the direct primary and a railroad taxation bill. Both of these efforts immediately became controversial and brought about significant opposition, especially among the state's senators, including both the Old Guard Democrats and Republicans. Railroads poured money and power into lobbying to stop La Follette's plans for reform, knowing that they faced unwanted regulation and increased taxes. The result was that most of La Follette's

U.S. congressman Robert La Follette was a vocal critic of political machines and supported such progressive reforms as women's suffrage and minimum wage. In 1924, La Follette carried Wisconsin and garnered 17 percent of the national popular vote as the Progressive Party's presidential candidate.

reform goals were crushed, failing to become law or reality in Wisconsin. La Follette's initial steps toward progressive reform had failed.

When he ran for reelection in 1902, La Follette renewed his efforts, fighting back hard against his opponents and appealing directly to the people of Wisconsin to support him and his agenda for reform. Again, La Follette was elected governor and, again, he tried to implement the direct primary and railroad control and taxation. This time, he managed to succeed with both. The direct primary law was not passed without a significant fight, however, and the railroad taxation bill passed only when the railroads shifted their resources against fighting regulation. On that score, the railroads managed to win, as Wisconsin did not see any significant railroad control. (La Follette had pushed for the creation of a railroad commission in his state to monitor railroad freight rates and service standards but lost that fight.)

La Follette was making inroads. Reelection loomed again in 1904, and the Wisconsin leader worked hard not only for reelection for himself, but for the election of legislative candidates who would help support his progressive agenda. Tirelessly, La Follette stumped across his state, speaking to countless audiences of voters. One of his favorite tactics was to remind his audiences of the voting records of Wisconsin legislators he wanted to see defeated in the election. He would then follow his recitation with the words "Put the men who have betrayed you on the retired list."[36] The challenge that La Follette represented to the state Republican organization and the railroads was as significant as ever, and these elements battled to keep La Follette from being nominated again for governor. When the governor was renominated anyway, party leaders tried to launch their own candidate but were blocked by the state Supreme Court. Frustrated, many of the party regulars left the Republican Party and supported the Democratic candidate. La Follette managed to squeak out a victory once more, but only by the narrowest of margins. This time as governor, though, he enjoyed the support of a newly elected Wisconsin House and Senate. With their backing, La Follette saw a new day for progressive reform in his state. In addition to his earlier successes, he pushed through new laws to support the establishment of a railroad commission with real power, registration for state lobbyists, and competitive civil service examinations for those who sought government jobs. The old party politics seemed to be a thing of the past. By 1906, a now nationally known Robert La Follette ran for the U.S. Senate and won.

5

Following La Follette

As Robert La Follette took up the call of the Progressive movement, the reach of America's reformers was extended. What had brought the movement about in the first place? What had prompted so many Americans to take up the banner of change and reform? In 1900, as the nation slipped into the new century, a new phase of American reform mindedness stood on the social horizon. Many of those who had opposed the development and power of labor unions and other reforms before and during the 1890s were gradually becoming convinced that there was a basic need for reform in American society. They had witnessed and were deeply affected by the tumultuous upheaval that had taken place on American farms and in urban factories, which had evolved into an ever-deepening class conflict.

By the turn of the century, many members of America's middle class were seeing the dangers before them. They began to realize the importance of reform and sought to bring about improvements in the conditions in which the underclass of Americans, including recent immigrants and minorities, especially blacks, lived. They believed that they needed to take positive steps on behalf of reform or else the more radical, socialist elements in the nation would take steps of their own. Moderate, middle-class would-be reformers feared that the nation might change too dramatically, thus resulting in a United States that was deeply radicalized. Almost all at once, these various reform interests joined together in a movement that has been labeled since by historians as Progressivism.

MOTIVATIONS FOR REFORM

Not all progressive reformers of the early twentieth century agreed in their individual social, political, and economic goals and concerns, but many shared some of the same fundamental beliefs. For one, these progressive reformers did not believe that the United States was on the verge of absolute catastrophe or imminent social collapse. The Progressives were, typically, patriotic Americans who were highly nationalistic and proud of their country. It was the existence of the American republic that served as a motivation for these reformers. They were actually optimistic about America's future: They thought that there was no better country in the world than the United States, but they were realistic enough to admit that America had serious problems. Those problems could be fixed in a democratic country where power was held by people who had a strong moral foundation. These critics of America were loyal citizens. With Progressivism, nationalism and reform could walk hand in hand. Everything was about the potential that America's ideals represented.

Despite their desire to bring about change in the American republic, most of the Progressives thought that change should come through gradual reform. The society that most of them lived in was a decent and reasonable one, and revolutionary actions would result only in the destruction of that society, not in its reform. Progressives were not interested in advancing any radical agenda such as socialism or anarchism. Instead, the march for progress would be based on change that occurred step by step with much forethought, planning, and design. Many of the Progressives were also motivated by their personal belief systems, especially by the value that they placed on their morality and dedication to service to their fellow citizens. Their strong moral frameworks made them optimistic about national issues that could be solved through ethical legislation.

These influences—their optimism, strong sense of morality, nationalistic pride, and foundational belief in American republicanism—helped to shape the Progressive agenda that took form during the first two decades of the twentieth century. That agenda would include goals such as ending American poverty, fighting injustice and the unregulated power of big business, preserving the country's national resources through conservation, and a call for a return to honest and efficient government. This agenda, the Progressives believed, could be achieved by using Christian ethics and morals in redesigning the American social fabric.

Some of these goals were also achieved through new approaches to America's problems. One was the Progressives' confidence in using "experts," including college and university professors, sociologists, economists, political scientists, social reformers, city planners, professional advisors, and city managers, to fix some of these problems. Such professionals could be relied on to provide fair, thoughtful, rational, and scientific methods and apply them to the issues and problems that faced the nation. The era gave rise to the establishment of legislative investigating commissions and other bodies at every level of government—city, local, state, and federal—who were equipped to isolate problems and suggest solutions. Progressives also supported the use of nonpartisan commissions or councils to run America's cities, thus

SUBSTANTIVE DUE PROCESS

As the fledgling Progressive movement began to expand, it met an almost immediate roadblock. Reform was sometimes held up by the American legal system, especially by judges who made decisions in support of America's business interests. The legal doctrine such judges used was referred to as "substantive due process," which gave "state and federal judges a way to block legislative attempts to regulate economic behavior."[*] The concept was simple: The Fourteenth Amendment to the U.S. Constitution, which had been added after the Civil War and which guaranteed due process to all Americans and their interests, should not be applied to interpreting a new law only on the basis of whether the procedure used to create the new act was fair or not. Judges also believed that they should weigh "whether the law was so inherently unfair that it would be unjust even if the procedures for implementing the statute was unbiased."[**] This view gave conservative, business-friendly judges the power to determine whether a law passed to regulate big business was fair to that business even if the intent of the law mirrored the public good.

Not all American judges agreed with this legal philosophy that supported large corporations. One was a Massachusetts jurist named Oliver Wendell Holmes, Jr. He was a conservative judge, who supported the will of the people (through the various legislatures) in legal decisions. He thought that it was important to view whether a law was rational and made good sense for the nation when determining its constitutionality. Another such American legal scholar was fellow Massachusetts legal mind Louis D. Brandeis. Through his view of the law, Brandeis would become known as "the People's Lawyer" because he argued that the American court system should represent the people, small businesses, and the nation's consumers just as much as the big corporations.

[*] Edward L. Ayers, *American Passages: A History of the United States* (Belmont, Calif.: Thomson Wadsworth, 2007), 558.
[**] Ibid.

eliminating the long-standing power of the city bosses and city machine government. Commissions became so commonplace that, by 1914, the independent commission form of municipal government had been installed in more than 400 American cities.

LA FOLLETTE'S REFORMS SPREAD ACROSS AMERICA

Robert La Follette's campaign to bring progressive reform to the state of Wisconsin would change politics dramatically both in his home state, and for the country at large. His political wins in Wisconsin became rallying posts for other reform-minded politicians in other states. Government could be bettered and positive legislation on behalf of the people could be passed by honest politicians dedicated to their constituencies. Everywhere, Americans spoke in support of something they called the "Wisconsin Idea," the concept that state government could be redirected, creating, in La Follette's words, "a happier and better state to live in, that its institutions are more democratic, that the opportunities of all its people are more equal, that social justice more nearly prevails, that human life is safer and sweeter."[37]

"GOLDEN RULE" JONES

Other politicians had been trying their hand at state political reform even before La Follette provided an example. In New York, Theodore Roosevelt, fresh from his exploits in the Spanish-American War in the summer of 1898, was elected governor of New York. During his campaign, Roosevelt publicly spoke out against the power held by some of America's largest corporations. Reform-minded politicians such as La Follette and Roosevelt

Elected governor of New York in 1898, Theodore Roosevelt was one of the first prominent Progressive politicians. He championed the conservation movement and opposed trusts such as Standard Oil, which controlled as much as 90 percent of the oil industry.

were among a tiny number of would-be reformers in the mid-to-late 1890s, and they represented the beginning of the reform movement that would become Progressivism. These reformers were some of the first to argue that significant reform in the United States would be possible only when the federal government decided to take a leading role to bring about nationwide change through the shaping of legislation to fight big business, curb the power of the railroads, and support social reform.

Those who provided leadership to the early Progressive movement included Samuel "Golden Rule" Jones of Toledo, a "big, fair-haired Welshman"[38] and factory owner. He began his progressive agenda inside his factory. It was embodied in a large sign that hung over his plant, taken from Scripture and words spoken by Jesus: "Therefore, whatsoever things ye would that men should do unto you, do ye even so to them." Jones first put his progressive ideas to work in his own factory. He paid his workers good wages for an eight-hour workday and provided vacation pay and profit sharing for his employees. He even supplied recreational and sports facilities for his workers to provide quality leisure activities.

In 1897, Samuel Jones was elected as a reform mayor of Toledo. He was as progressive on behalf of the city as he was with his factory employees. He campaigned for school reform and new school facilities, as well as for parks and recreation areas across the city. He refused to play the usual politics of offering city contracts in exchange for political support, but he did fight for a strong civil service program for Toledo. The progressive mayor established city control over the trolley system, and he improved the wages of municipal workers so that they were paid more than an average industrial worker. Jones also established a system of kindergarten schools for young children.

Such moves by Toledo's mayor were popular with many of his voters, but he had other ideas and positions that were less acceptable. He thought that all utility companies should be publicly, not privately, owned. To make police work more humane, he ordered the city's policemen not to carry nightsticks. Sometimes, when "he sat as a magistrate, he preferred to lecture offenders and then release them."[39] Such practices and positions caused party bosses to turn on him and refuse to support him for reelection in 1899. Jones bypassed party leaders and won another mayoral term as an independent. He was elected to the mayorship four more times and died in office in 1904.

ANOTHER OHIO PROGRESSIVE

Just as progressive Ohioans enjoyed the leadership of Jones in Toledo, another Ohio city also reaped the benefits of an important progressive politician. Tom L. Johnson, like Jones, was a factory owner and industrialist in Cleveland. Given his early career, he was an unlikely candidate for the causes of the Progressive movement. Johnson was born south of the Ohio River, in Kentucky, as the son of a slave owner. He had little education growing up and became both a self-taught mechanic and bookkeeper. Then, while working for the Louisville Street Railway Company, his inventive mind created a new type of fare box that would be used on the streetcars, trolleys, and, later, buses. This single invention made Johnson wealthy. In time, he not only worked for a streetcar company, he was buying such companies in Cleveland, Indianapolis, Detroit, and New York City. Like so many of his day, Johnson was a merciless and intelligent businessman.

Then, one day, Johnson's life changed. While on a train ride, he bought a book, written by Progressive economist and social thinker Henry George, from a newsboy. The book was titled *Social Problems*. George's book, like an earlier work—*Progress and Poverty*—was concerned with social issues, especially how to limit the accumulation of wealth at the expense of the working class. George believed that, whenever there is an increase in wealth for the few, there is an increase in poverty for the poor. Johnson was touched by George's writing and became a would-be Progressive in short order. (He would later support George's campaign

In his 1879 book *Progress and Poverty*, economist Henry George proposed that landowners and monopolists were the main cause of poverty in the United States, because they accumulated too much wealth and did not distribute enough of it to their workers. Ironically, George finished ahead of Theodore Roosevelt in New York City's 1886 mayoral election but lost to Democrat Abram Stevens Hewitt.

to become mayor of New York, a bid that failed.) Johnson went into politics himself, serving two terms in the House of Representatives. He would eventually sell off his business assets and spend the remainder of his life trying to serve the public as a Progressive reformer.

This was a role he would fulfill after his election as mayor of Cleveland in 1901. The moneyed interests did not campaign against him, thinking that he was a safe politician because he was wealthy. Johnson surprised them: He made moves that were extremely popular with the people of the city of Cleveland, including lowering streetcar fares and introducing "an electric lighting plan to show how rates could be kept low."[40]

One of Johnson's important goals was to institutionalize city ownership of utility companies. He, of course, had personal experience in this arena as a former owner of mass transit companies. "I believe in municipal ownership of all public service monopolies," Johnson explained, "for the same reason that I believe in the municipal ownership of waterworks, of parks, of schools. I believe in the municipal ownership of these monopolies because if you do not own them they will in time own you. They will rule your politics, corrupt your institutions and finally destroy your liberties."[41]

Mayor Johnson achieved nearly all of his progressive goals in a relatively short period of time. He did not put his entire program in place all at once but rather implemented it in stages, beginning with taxing the lands and properties owned by public service companies. The results of his efforts on behalf of the city of Cleveland were obvious and clear to everyone, whether they supported his causes or not:

> Johnson shook out the time-servers and filled their places with energetic determined and idealistic men. A clergy man became chief of prisons and charities, a shrewd young lawyer became city solicitor and a former professor of economics was brought in from New York to help with tax assessments. In short order the city's services were being performed more efficiently and petty corruption was practically at an end. An experienced journalist who visited Cleveland pronounced it the best-governed city in America.[42]

Mayor Johnson remained at the helm of Cleveland's municipal government until 1909, when he was finally defeated in a reelection bid. Johnson, like La Follette and other early Progressives, had made his contributions to the cause and "had inspired men all over the country to believe that government could help the public to protect itself against the economic aristocracy."[43]

THE PENS OF PROGRESSIVISM

The likes of La Follette, Johnson, and Jones managed to bring direction to their progressive agendas in their respective cities and states. There would be others like them, including Albert B. Cummins in Iowa and Hiram Johnson in California, whose reforms would spread across their states, both through the Republican Party. In other states, including North Dakota, Missouri, and Minnesota, Democratic reformers would lead the battle for Progressivism. Reforms spread across the country, from state to state, as governors, legislators, and street-level movements pushed to enact reforms such as the direct primary; referendum and initiative laws; tax reforms; utility and railroad regulation; and a host of other causes. Their intention was to create a better government that served the people, while reining in power held by private corporations and individuals with personal economic power.

Newspapers were sometimes willing allies to the politicians intent on reform. Daily and weekly newspapers touched the lives of the vast majority of Americans. This mass circulation of information managed to play a significant role in the advancement of the progressive agenda. Progressivism was a hot topic, and "enterprising publishers, ever on the lookout for circulation-building stories, scented a profitable field for investigation."[44]

Two of the most influential newspaper moguls of the 1890s and early twentieth century were William Randolph Hearst and Joseph Pulitzer. Both publishers owned multiple newspapers that circulated across the country, but their main city of competition was New York, where Hearst published the *New York Journal*. These leading newspapermen published an endless stream of articles, features, and news stories on a wide variety of Progressive topics; however, the newspapers of the day were heavy on sensationalism and exploitation. Often, the angles that editors took focused on exposés intended to excite the public. Hearst was a constant critic of the railroads, especially the Southern Pacific (formerly the California-based Central Pacific, which had constructed a portion of the nation's first transcontinental railroad line), producing a constant drumbeat against high railroad rates and the ways that the railroads regularly bribed public officials. He also campaigned against the abuses of public utilities and business monopolies and sided with workers concerning labor issues. In time, Hearst used the popularity he had gained through his newspaper work to run for president of the United States, an effort that failed miserably in 1904. Other campaigns to become New York's governor and mayor of New York City also failed. In time, he even cooled on some of his progressive agendas.

For all of his excesses and sensational journalism, Hearst managed to inspire a generation of journalists who were serious opponents of the national abuses that were so often targeted by Progressives. The primary contribution of these newspaper and magazine writers was made through use of the exposé, an article that revealed a problem that needed to be addressed, whether a national issue or one isolated to a specific city or state. Most of the work of this small cadre of writers took place after 1902, during the early years of the presidency of New Yorker Theodore Roosevelt. Roosevelt would give these journalists and writers a label that would remain with them through the period of Progressivism: muckrakers.

One of the prominent muckrakers (investigative reporters) of the Progressive era, Ida Tarbell (*above*) opposed trusts because she believed that they used unfair practices to drive smaller companies out of business. In 1904, she wrote the *History of the Standard Oil Company*, which ultimately helped break the Standard Oil monopoly.

Roosevelt first used the label in 1906 to identify this important group of Progressive penmen and -women. He originally meant the term to be derogatory, stating that these writers reminded him of a character in John Bunyan's novel *Pilgrim's Progress*, the Man with the Muck-rake, who filtered through dung and filth in search of a heavenly crown. Roosevelt's "muckraker" reference would be taken on by the writers he was referring to, and they turned it into a crown of sorts of their own. (Roosevelt had actually been referring to some of the more sensational writers among those who published progressive exposés.)

Muckrakers wrote for the newspapers, and they made their most important marks through the popular magazines of the period, monthly publications that included *Munsey's*, *Cosmopolitan*, and *McClure's*. Such magazines enjoyed wide circulations, not just for publishing political exposés, but for their popular fiction, including the writings of Mark Twain, Robert Louis Stevenson, Jack London, and Rudyard Kipling.

Chief among the magazine-publishing Progressives was S. S. McClure. He was one of the earliest monthly publishers to see the commercial advantages of printing exposés and other features that revealed the need for reform. McClure hired several good writers who could turn a story with a journalistic hand, making a subject readable and, thus, accessible to a wide audience. Two of his best hires were Ida M. Tarbell and Lincoln Steffens. They came to *McClure's* as writers of reputation with proven track records of publishing, editing, and journalistic investigating. Tarbell was skilled in historical research, and Steffens, from California but educated in Europe, was a former New York newspaper editor. When he was hired by McClure, Steffens believed it was as an editor. The wily McClure sent him out to work as a reporter and investigator. "You may have been an editor," he told Steffens, "but you don't know how to edit a magazine. . . . Get out of here, travel, go—somewhere. . . . Buy a railroad ticket, get on a train, and there, where it lands you, there you will learn to edit a magazine."[45] McClure wanted Steffens to work as a reporter, and he would become one of the best in the business.

Steffens boarded a train and traveled around the country, landing in Missouri, where he found the story McClure told him to find in St. Louis. The city had only recently been rocked by a public scandal exposed by a young prosecuting attorney. Joseph Folk had taken several city aldermen to court, where they were convicted of taking bribes from some of the city's wealthy citizens. Steffens, working alongside a local St. Louis reporter, Claude H. Wetmore, wrote up the lurid story of big-city corruption. McClure ran the series of articles in his magazine beginning in October 1902, with an article entitled "Tweed Days in St. Louis." In time, Steffens would have his work published in a book entitled *Shame of the Cities*.

Just a month after Steffens published his first article on municipal corruption in St. Louis, Ida Tarbell published the first of her most important muckraking articles, one on the history of Standard Oil Company. One of the important goals of the Progressives was to attack big businesses that were nothing more than monopolies, companies that controlled the vast majority of the business of a single commodity. Examples ran from rubber to chemicals to sugar to tobacco to oil. These monopolies were usually called trusts. One such "trust" was the company that had been formed through the overbearing capitalism of oil tycoon John Rockefeller. His company, Standard Oil, controlled as much as 90 percent of the oil industry in the United States at the beginning of the twentieth century.

Tarbell's series on Rockefeller and his oil empire was a professional and personal effort. Her father was a small-time oilman who had been driven out of business by Rockefeller's expansive tactics. She spent years researching historical documents, conducting endless interviews, and reading a mountain of official reports. She even spoke with Standard Oil officials to gather the information she would turn into one of the most important series of muckraking articles of the early 1900s. Before she was finished, Tarbell exposed Rockefeller and his company for doing business

Trusts such as Standard Oil held monopolies over their particular industry, which not only limited competition but drove up prices. The owners of these trusts, such as Standard Oil president John D. Rockefeller, who is depicted in this cartoon titled "King of the World," often wielded great power and influence.

that included bribing government officials while ruthlessly destroying smaller and competing oil companies.

Such work by Steffens, Tarbell, and others who wrote for McClure gained a wide public readership. Their works, along with those of other journalistic muckrakers, such as Ray Stannard Baker, would boost the sales of *McClure's* dramatically. Soon, many other magazines were busy copying this same style of journalism. Unscrupulous insurance companies, Wall Street investors, the meatpacking industry, and the patent medicine industry— all were fair game for the pens of the muckrakers. Even some of the more genteel magazines of the day—*Ladies' Home Journal, Collier's,* and others—published stories and features that pushed the progressive agenda. In the pages of *Cosmopolitan,* writer David Graham Phillips published a series that exposed corruption in the very halls of the United States Senate. His series, *The Treason of the Senate,* revealed graft on a grand scale among those who held some of the highest offices in the land. Eventually, Progressives would succeed in bringing about the passage of the Seventeenth Amendment to the Constitution, which established the direct election of U.S. senators, rather than having them selected by state legislators.

The impact that the muckrakers had on the general American public was without precedence. The early twentieth century in the United States was beginning with a spirit and initiative, led by individuals and organizations that were bent on bettering the country and its society. The Progressive movement was taking root, finding sympathetic supporters and angry advocates who were having an impact in the halls of city government, state houses, and even national leadership. As the movement made its early efforts and found traction through the labors of many key figures whose constituencies and readers rallied around them, it existed for several years without a single national figure to provide its leadership and help set its agenda. That crucial figure in the movement, however, would soon find his way to the national stage through the White House—Theodore Roosevelt.

6

Roosevelt's Progressivism

New Yorker Theodore Roosevelt was thrust onto the national stage in 1901 with the firing of an assassin's gun. In 1900, the Republican Party renominated its then-standing president, William McKinley. McKinley had first been elected in 1896, when he defeated William Jennings Bryan, who was both the Democratic and the Populist candidate that year. The party dropped its vice president, Garret A. Hobart, in 1900 and instead chose a war hero, fresh from the short conflict that had erupted in the spring and summer of 1898 between the United States and Spain. Theodore Roosevelt had resigned his post as assistant secretary of the navy, generally an unimportant government position, to rush into the war before it was over. He raised a unit of volunteer cavalry troops that included old Harvard buddies and cowboys he had met out West when he tried his hand at cattle ranching during the 1880s. Roosevelt's Rough Riders had found action in Cuba, fighting their way up Kettle and San Juan hills, bringing Roosevelt fame and political clout. The party tacked him onto the McKinley ticket, and out went Vice President Hobart.

ROOSEVELT TAKES THE LEAD

The newly elected ticket of McKinley and Roosevelt did not last long. In September 1901, McKinley was fatally shot while attending a World's Fair in Buffalo, New York. With McKinley's death, Roosevelt, then in his early 40s, suddenly found himself president of the United States. When he first gained the highest office in the land—he would refer to the presidency as his "bully pulpit"—Roosevelt indicated publicly that "he would carry forward the late President McKinley's policies."[46] McKinley had not, in general, been a part of the Progressive movement and had been a fairly conservative president who was a friend to big business. With Roosevelt's initial assurances, the nation's financial leaders and industrial giants believed that they had little to fear from him as a potential supporter of Progressivism. They should have known better.

Roosevelt had already served in politics beginning in the late 1890s, and his track record as a state congressman, a civil service commissioner, New York City police superintendent, and New York governor had often supported, at least in spirit, some of the elements of the Progressives. He was, after all, a man of action. He was an avid reader, writer, and thinker who published books on a variety of subjects, primarily history. He had studied botany and natural science and loved the great outdoors, enjoying hunting as a sport. Roosevelt was extremely physical, taking on the challenges of boxing and gymnastics as a young boy, even though he struggled with asthma. For a couple of years, he spent time in North Dakota where he bought and ran a cattle ranch, taking on the persona and character of an American cowboy. He had turned to politics by the late 1880s, when he made the decision to "be one of the governing class"[47] and joined the Republican Club in his New York City district. Although he held several political offices, he failed to win the mayoral seat of New York City. Through his experiences in politics, though, whether win or lose, he had spent years learning the ropes of leadership, as well as "how to work the levers that made governmental machinery move."[48] Before leaving the White House, Roosevelt would not only advance the Progressive cause, he would redefine the role of an American president.

Taking the office in the fall of 1901, he took few steps that would have been out of line even for someone as conservative as McKinley. Only his invitation to host Booker

Shortly after becoming president in 1901, Theodore Roosevelt set out to regulate the trusts. Here, Roosevelt is depicted in a cartoon from the *Evening Star*, which illustrates his penchant for determining which trusts should be destroyed and which should merely be shackled.

T. Washington, one of the nation's most important black leaders at that time, at a White House dinner managed to raise a few Southern eyebrows.

Less than six months into his presidency, however, Roosevelt was taking bold steps that were lauded by the supporters of Progressivism. He set out to break up a large corporation that he considered nothing short of a trust. The president ordered his attorney general, Philander Knox,

AN END TO CORPORATE REBATES

During his first two years in office, President Roosevelt took many bold steps against what he considered questionable and even illegal practices of large corporations. One of his first attempts to break up a corporation was the suit the U.S. Justice Department filed against a major railroad conglomerate, Northern Securities. A majority of the general public had come to despise the business practices of many of the country's railroads. Farmers and other users of the railroads were especially irate about the practice of rebates. By the early twentieth century, however, rebates were considered bad business even by some of the same corporate interests that had previously made use of the practice.

The purpose of such corporate rebates, as practiced by the railroads, was to officially charge a given customer a freight rate that was publicly known and published, the rate charged to everyone else. Secretly, though, the railroads would later hand back a portion of the official freight rate to its largest corporate customers to encourage those companies to use the railroads. One such company that profited from this arrangement was Rockefeller's Standard Oil Company. When Ida Tarbell wrote her exposé on the massive oil company's practices, she publicized the fact that Standard Oil had regularly received rebates on the freight rates it had paid to a number of railroad companies. In the meantime, Rockefeller's competitors had paid the same public rate but did not receive rebates. This unfair practice had helped push some of Rockefeller's competitors

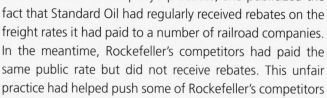

to file a suit against the Northern Securities Company, a large holding company established by Wall Street investor J. Pierpont Morgan and railroad tycoon Edward H. Harriman. The company held control of several railroad companies under one financial roof, thus dramatically reducing the level of competition among them. To Roosevelt, the very existence of the Northern Securities Company was a violation of the Sherman Antitrust Act, which had been passed in Congress

out of business. This, of course, resulted in a decline in competition in the oil industry.

By the turn of the twentieth century, the practice was common in the marketplace. It had developed into a complicated mathematical system that included sliding scales from one industry to the next. This would become part of the problem that would lead to an opposition to rebates even among corporations themselves. For example, according to a report made by Governor Robert La Follette of Wisconsin, one of his state's manufacturing firms had regularly received 50¢ back for every $1.50 it paid in freight rates. The Wisconsin factory owner was pleased with the arrangement until he realized that one of his competitors was receiving a rebate of 65¢. This competition for rebates would finally lead corporate leaders to decide that the practice of rebates probably did more harm than good, even for themselves. Ironically, even the railroad companies agreed.

Perhaps more ironic, the congressional sponsor of the act that Roosevelt wanted passed to declare rebates illegal was a Republican connected to the business world. He was very wealthy and extremely conservative—West Virginia senator Stephen B. Elkins. When he brought the proposed legislation to Congress, it passed almost immediately. Rebates had become unpopular, even to businesses that had thrived on them in early times.

in 1890 as the "first attempt at national regulation of trusts, combinations, and monopolies."[49]

BATTLING MORGAN

J. Pierpont Morgan was one of the richest men in the United States, and he was shocked when President Roosevelt made charges against one of his companies. (He was dining at home when he received word by telephone.) Morgan was disappointed in Roosevelt, having thought "Roosevelt to be a gentleman, but a gentleman would not have sued."[50] Earlier presidents had left him alone, allowing him to pursue his business and financial interests without government intrusion. The angry New York tycoon wanted to settle the issue between himself and the president. "If we have done anything wrong," Morgan communicated to Roosevelt, "send your man to my man and they can fix it up."[51] Morgan believed that things could be handled in a friendly manner between one of his lawyers and Roosevelt's attorney general. Roosevelt was not interested in working out a "deal" with J. P. Morgan, however: He wanted to break up Northern Securities, and that was all that mattered. To the president, it was a simple matter of enforcing the laws that were intended to regulate big business interests. His message was clear: "that there were limits to what the government would let men do in using the mechanism of the holding company to build up economic empires."[52]

When it became clear to Morgan that President Roosevelt did not intend to back down on his claim against Northern Securities, the Wall Street banker nearly panicked. "Are you going to attack my other interests, the Steel Trust and the others?" he asked. Roosevelt's response was reassuring: "Certainly not, unless we find that in any case they have done something that we regard as wrong."[53] Newspaper publisher Joseph Pulitzer was excited. He applauded Roosevelt, believing that the president had "subjugated Wall Street."[54] It was a new day for Progressivism.

The demise of the Northern Securities Company did not take place overnight. The legal system moved along slowly until the U.S. Supreme Court agreed on March 14, 1904, that the company should be broken up, voting 5 to 4 in favor of that measure. Newly appointed justice Oliver Wendell Holmes, Jr., who brought to the high court a legal view that the Constitution should be interpreted more flexibly, supported a position that bolstered the work of the Progressives. Holmes did not vote with the majority of the court on this case, however.

The importance of the Northern Securities decision was that it reestablished the power of the government to enforce the Sherman Antitrust Act, a power that had fallen into question after an 1895 Supreme Court decision that had weakened the government's role. Other antitrust suits would follow the success of the Northern Securities case. Roosevelt next targeted the meatpackers' trust. Again, his justice department won its case. In all, the Roosevelt administration would file more than 40 antitrust suits against major companies across the United States. (Perhaps with great political cleverness, Roosevelt did not order another antitrust suit filed after the Beef Trust case until after the 1904 congressional elections. He did not want to hurt Republican candidates and their chances for reelection.) Nevertheless, Roosevelt would soon gain the reputation of being a "trustbuster."

SETTLING A MINERS' STRIKE

Roosevelt also supported other Progressive measures. The president's support of national conservation of America's natural resources led him to push the Newlands Act, also known as the Reclamation Act, through Congress. This act gave the federal government the authority to build irrigation projects and large dams for the purpose of providing water for land reclamation on arid stretches of the West.

When 140,000 members of the United Mine Workers walked off their jobs in Pennsylvania, calling for a coal

One of Theodore Roosevelt's most important accomplishments during his presidency was brokering a deal between the United Mine Workers and labor leaders during the anthracite coal strike of 1902. At the time, Americans relied on coal to heat their homes, and Roosevelt, with the help of his strike arbitration committee (*pictured here*), was able to convince the miners to return to work before winter arrived.

mining strike, Roosevelt took an immediate interest. Such strikes, whether in mining, railroads, steel mills, or other arenas of American production, had previously been met by presidents who supported the industry owners and forced the workers back to work, sometimes under the threat of the military. This strike was quite extensive, and it threatened to be a long labor battle, one that might leave the nation short on coal supplies with the approach of the winter of 1902–1903. Roosevelt felt that he had to intervene.

The results of the government's involvement broke new ground. Roosevelt ordered representatives of both labor and management to come to the White House to sit down together to work out an agreement. When an agreement was slow in coming, Roosevelt threatened to send in the military to take over and work the coal mines themselves. Ironically, with help from J. Pierpont Morgan, the president formed a commission to examine both sides in the labor dispute. The commission's recommendation was to give the miners a 10 percent increase in pay. This time, an American president was dealing with both labor and management in the same way, refusing to take a strong side with one over the other. It was something new for labor, a fair approach by an American president that Roosevelt himself would soon call his "Square Deal."[55]

FURTHER PROGRESSIVE MEASURES

Roosevelt would take additional steps to bolster his progressive policies. In 1902, he encouraged Congress to pass the Elkins Act, which made it illegal for railroads to kick back rebates to their favored, large-scale customers while charging small haulers, such as farmers, the standard higher rate. It was a bright day for farmers. Roosevelt supported the creation of a cabinet-level bureaucracy, the Department of Commerce and Labor. Within this department was the Bureau of Corporations, which was given the power to make corporations' records public and to determine which companies were abusing power in the marketplace. The Elkins Act, the measure to create the Department of Commerce and Labor, and another new law, the Expedition Act (its purpose was to streamline the process for prosecuting cases against monopolies), were all passed by Congress on the same day—February 19, 1903.

Such steps on the part of the president might have antagonized and alarmed the more conservative members of his political party, but Roosevelt soon convinced his wary opponents that he did not intend to take further steps to advance the progressive agenda. His attorney general, Philander Knox, informed the cautious members of Congress that, with the passage of the Elkins Act and the Expedition Act, "the Congress has now enacted all that is practicable and all that is desirable to do" for Progressivism.[56] For the remainder of his first term as president—from the spring of 1903 until the election in November of the following year—Roosevelt did little on behalf of a Progressive agenda. He actually spent much of his time retooling the U.S. military, reforming the army's administration by creating a general staff, and making other changes, including restructuring the National Guard. Such moves made few waves other than with old-line military personnel. Businessmen across the United States breathed a sigh of relief. Perhaps President Roosevelt had managed to throw off his earlier support of the Progressive agenda. He had, after all, not really made any true radical steps. He was, at best, a "mild progressive."[57]

Roosevelt continued to make deft moves as president, though, moves that were slowly defining him as an active, engaged leader. With few exceptions during the previous 30 years, Republican presidents (only one Democrat president was elected between 1860 and 1900—Grover Cleveland) had managed to serve by taking their lead from Congress, satisfied to be led rather than to truly lead. Roosevelt was nursing other approaches as president. He was a mover and shaker, a national figure who chose his own direction and expected others to follow him. His approach would redefine the modern presidency; it would also continue to serve him in his later support of more progressive agendas. He wanted to accomplish certain things for the American public, but they would have to wait until after the 1904 election.

For a brief moment, Roosevelt thought that he might face a serious challenge for the Republican nomination for president in 1904. When his chief rival, Mark Hanna, suddenly died of typhoid fever in February of that year, it was clear that Roosevelt would have no problem receiving his party's endorsement as their standard bearer in 1904. In 1901, Roosevelt had inherited the presidency after the death of William McKinley. He would win it in his own right when he received the largest percentage of the national vote of any presidential candidate to that date (7.63 million votes to the 5.1 million received by his Democrat challenger, Judge Alton B. Parker) in the election that brought him a second term in the White House.

7

The Roosevelt Legacy Continues

Roosevelt's second term would prove even more interesting than his first had been. Having put the election behind him, Roosevelt did not have to worry about whether his political steps were too progressive for his critics or the American people. He wasted no time in letting everyone know that he had a full agenda for the country. Even before his second inauguration, in January 1905, Roosevelt spoke to the Union League Club in Philadelphia in a speech in which he threw down the gauntlet. He had shelved his progressive tendencies for more than 18 months before the election, but he was now ready for new legislative action. His second term would break new ground, as he informed his Philadelphia audience:

> Unquestionably . . . the great development of industrialism means that there must be an increase in the supervision exercised by the Government over business enterprises. . . . Neither this people nor any other free people will permanently tolerate the use of the vast power conferred by vast wealth, and especially by wealth in its corporate form, without lodging somewhere in the Government the still higher power of seeing that this power, in addition to being used in the interest of the individual or individuals possessing it, is also used for and not against the interests of the people as a whole. . . . No

finally satisfactory result can be expected from merely State action. The action must come through the Federal Government.[58]

PRESIDENTIAL VOICE OF PROGRESSIVISM

An eager and determined Roosevelt set out to bring to reality what he spoke of in theory. He soon called for new regulations on railroad freight rates; this concept was not new (similar laws had been in place on the state level for several decades, and Congress had created the Interstate Commerce Commission [ICC] back in 1887 to regulate rail rates), but Roosevelt's initiative was one of the first on a national scale with clout. His proposal was to strengthen the 1887 ICC law, granting real power to the commission to establish a maximum ceiling on freight rates. Although this was a narrow move made by Roosevelt, it sent howls throughout the business world.

Conservatives across the country soon joined the chorus. Railroads were big business in the United States, a steel-based foundation to the nation's economy. They did not believe in the power of government being used to limit the capacity of business to operate at its full potential and thought that government "intrusion" would only hamper the national economy. Such conservatives even felt that government control might border on the immoral because, in their view, the government was dictating "how owners of property should use their property."[59] But, despite attempts made by congressional conservatives to stop Roosevelt's plan, the president pushed his legislation forward. He was careful to inform critics of his plan that his proposal would provide railroad officials an opportunity, through government hearings, to explain and justify any and all freight rate increases. This only defused the conflict slightly, however.

(continues on page 90)

ROOSEVELT VS. ALDRICH: A BATTLE OF POWER

As President Theodore Roosevelt attempted to create new progressive laws for America, he sometimes found himself facing serious opposition. The progressive agenda was not universally supported during the early years of the twentieth century, and even the president of the United States was sometimes forced to make concessions and political deals to get at least some of his progressive goals achieved. Forceful politicians such as Senator Nelson Aldrich stood in the way of Roosevelt.

When Theodore Roosevelt became president in 1901, Aldrich had already been a U.S. senator for 20 years. Raised in Rhode Island, Aldrich came from simple roots, having worked as a young delivery boy who only later made himself rich by selling streetcar franchises. He became wealthy, rubbing shoulders with the likes of John D. Rockefeller and J. Pierpont Morgan, with whom he went yachting. By the time he was elected to the U.S. Senate, Aldrich was a skilled and persuasive salesman, a man "who measured his opponents, credited them with maximum skill, and still outthought them."[*] Even a politician as intelligent as Roosevelt found Aldrich to be a singular challenge as an opponent.

When Roosevelt's railroad regulation—it would become the Hepburn Act—cleared the House of Representatives in the spring of 1905, the bill reached the Senate and everyone, including the president, anticipated opposition from the senior senator from Rhode Island. Some anticipated a move by Aldrich through the Committee on Interstate and Foreign Commerce, but Senator Aldrich made no overt moves against the bill. The 13-person committee was dominated by eight Republicans. As the committee met, its members kept waiting for Aldrich to send proposed amendments to the railroad control bill, changes that they expected would water down or even kill its chances for passage. Senator Aldrich said little, however, remaining quiet at the committee table "in almost Buddha-like calm."[**] Some senators even began to consider that the proposed Hepburn Bill would make it through the Senate without any opposition from Aldrich. They would soon discover they were wrong.

Just as the bill was nearing its final, accepted form, Aldrich made his move. He proposed that each member of the committee be allowed to introduce amendments, not during committee meetings, but on the floor of the Senate itself, before the entire membership of the congressional body. Roosevelt and his supporters smelled a problem, but Aldrich's resolution passed. Aldrich wasted no time in making his second move against the Hepburn bill. Through Aldrich's control over the committee, a Democratic senator—"Pitchfork Ben" Tillman from South Carolina—was selected to officiate over the debate of the bill in the Senate. This move ensured that the Republicans would not control the debate and that, if the bill passed, it would not be seen as an entirely Republican success at the expense of the Democratic Party. Roosevelt and his supporters were immediately alarmed. The bill would glide through the Senate, but every part of the bill might be picked apart, effectively killing the proposed legislation. Aldrich was now in control.

Days of debate soon opened on the Senate floor. Roosevelt tried to regain control of the process by seeking support from "a coalition of Bryan Democrats, progressives and regular Republicans."*** Fearing that he might not get his bill passed in its original form, Roosevelt even accepted a more radical form of the bill supported by several Democrats. Ironically, this different form of the bill did not gain enough support from the Democrats and failed. By compromising, Roosevelt found that he had lost some Republican votes. Things began to look dim for the passage of the Hepburn Act. The president was uncertain of his success on the issue, and Aldrich looked as though he would emerge as the winner of the titanic struggle over the legislation.

Then, at the last minute, events took a sudden and almost inexplicable turn. Somehow, President Roosevelt and Senator Aldrich managed to come to an agreement. (The written record and personal papers of both politicians do not adequately explain how the two men finally came to a consensus.) Roosevelt turned away from the more radical

(continues)

(continued)

rewriting of his regulatory legislation, and Aldrich allowed the bill to pass through the Senate unimpeded. It became law in May 1906. After months of debate, rewording, rewriting, and political horse trading, the Hepburn Act had finally passed, having changed little from its original wording.

* Ernest R. May, *The Progressive Era*, vol. 9, *1901–1917* (New York: Time Incorporated, 1964), 78.

** Ibid., 79.

*** Ibid.

(continued from page 87)

By early 1905, President Roosevelt had managed to see his legislation through the House of Representatives. The real battle royal was in the Senate. There, Roosevelt's primary opponent was millionaire Nelson W. Aldrich, a long-standing and powerful senator (he had first been elected to the Senate in 1881) who was a close friend of big business. He sailed regularly with J. Pierpont Morgan, and his son-in-law was John D. Rockefeller, Jr. The tone of the times was against an older politician such as Aldrich, however. Progressives in the Senate—including Democrats and Republicans, such as Senator La Follette from Wisconsin—banded together to help see the railroad legislation, known as the Hepburn Act, become law in the spring of 1906. It was altered little from what Roosevelt had sent to the House a year earlier.

This was only the beginning of government regulation on American business and commerce. Already, the investigative muckrakers of the Roosevelt era had made public the ineffectiveness of many patent medicines sold in drugstores across the country. Some simply did not work as they were advertised, and the content of others was dangerous, perhaps even lethal. A parallel campaign launched through the U.S. Department of Agriculture, led by Dr. Harvey Wiley, revealed that many factory-produced foods contained dangerous chemicals and other toxins that made them unsafe for human consumption. By the early spring of 1906, the Roosevelt administration had placed another bill on Congress's desk to create a law that would limit the sale of both food and medicines that could harm those who used them.

REGULATION AND CONSERVATION

At the same time, a work of fiction entered the political arena that soon had an impact on proposed legislation. In the winter of 1906, a novel by socialist writer Upton Sinclair reached American bookshelves. The book was entitled *The Jungle*, and it was a story set against the backdrop of American meatpacking plants. In his novel, Sinclair revealed the horrible conditions under which meat was packaged for human consumption. Although Sinclair's purpose was to shock people, he had not strayed far from the truth. Such plants were often filthy, with toxic chemicals, animal waste, and other contaminants finding their way into America's manufactured meat supply. Sinclair drove his basic message home hard: He wanted to gain support for the idea of government ownership of private meatpacking plants and the socialization of the means of production in the United States. Sinclair was, after all, a hard-shell socialist.

Roosevelt read the book and was just as outraged with its content as the American public was. He was not interested in Sinclair's socialist agenda, however. To swing wide of Sinclair's political goals, Roosevelt actively sought a change in the authority of the federal government's Department of Agriculture. He wanted to have the government establish a regulatory system to allow for

In 1906, author Upton Sinclair (*above*) published *The Jungle*, which revealed the terrible conditions in the meatpacking plants of Chicago's Union Stock Yards. Read by Theodore Roosevelt, Sinclair's novel was instrumental in convincing the president to regulate the agricultural industry.

federal inspection of meatpacking plants. Although the industry fought the legislation, Congress cooperated with Roosevelt by passing the Pure Food and Drug Act on June

30, 1906. In all, the act established three regulatory laws that the president considered "a noteworthy advance in the policy of securing Federal supervision and control over corporations."[60]

The president continued to support a progressive agenda throughout his presidency, and conservation measures were an important part of that agenda. During his first term, back in 1902, Roosevelt had pushed a bill through Congress that would become the Newlands Act. This important conservation measure authorized federal money for the construction of dams and other water reclamation projects, especially across the American West. The following year, he helped establish the first wildlife refuge in America. An avid bird enthusiast since he was a boy, Roosevelt established, by executive order, 51 bird sanctuaries and reservations across the country, including Florida's Pelican Island, his first, in 1903.

In his second term, Roosevelt placed federal lands under government protection by declaring them to have special scientific or historic interest under the Antiquities Act of 1906; these lands included Arizona's Petrified Forest and Grand Canyon, and Wyoming's Devils Tower. In 1907, Roosevelt signed an executive order to authorize the conversion of millions of acres of forest land in several western states into national reserves. He also withdrew additional lands, federal properties that contained valuable natural resources including coal, oil reserves, and mineral lands, from private sale. When Roosevelt took office, fewer than 50 million acres of federal lands had been designated as national forests. He would quadruple that acreage by the time he left office. During his presidency, he doubled the number of national parks. In 1906, Roosevelt made sure that the Yosemite Valley in northern California was turned over to the care of the federal government. Twelve-hundred square miles of monumental mountains, verdant valleys, grand waterfalls, and teeming forests of giant sequoias and redwoods were designated a national park.

During the final two years of his second term (1907–1909), he gave his support to and sometimes sponsored legislation for federal-level income taxes, as well as inheritance taxes, the eight-hour workday, the licensing of American corporations that engaged in interstate commerce, and the criminalization of violations of antitrust legislation, unfair labor practices, and questionable control of the stock market for personal gain by major investors. In his earlier presidential years, Roosevelt had pursued less bold ventures on behalf of Progressivism. For that, he was sometimes criticized by more radical Progressive leaders, such as Robert La Follette. As his presidency drew closer to its final days, though, Roosevelt supported increasingly dramatic elements of Progressivism.

A MILDER FORM OF PROGRESSIVISM

President Roosevelt may have been an important advocate for Progressive change during his presidency, but one reason that he gave his support to the political movement was that it allowed him to help set the movement's agenda. The early years of the twentieth century in America gave rise to several radical political theories and philosophies, including socialism. The Socialist Party was gaining votes in nearly every election, and this political extremism worried Roosevelt. He was opposed to the most radical element of the Socialist Party, which supported an extreme labor movement known as the Industrial Workers of the World (IWW). The group was established in 1905 and was inspired by the theories of the father of modern communism, German thinker Karl Marx. The IWW, popularly known as "the Wobblies," sought the overthrow of capitalism and

Pictured here shortly before the end of his second term in office, President Theodore Roosevelt hoped that his secretary of war, William Howard Taft, would continue to carry out his Progressive policies when he became president in 1908. Unfortunately for Roosevelt, Taft had other ideas.

the establishment of an American socialist state. Roosevelt might criticize the excesses of capitalism, but he did not wish to see it ended in the United States.

Despite Roosevelt's support of a milder form of Progressivism than that preached by the Socialists, he found himself criticized for his call for greater government control over the U.S. economy and capitalist abuses. Conservatives—many within his party—constantly spoke out against him. Such conservative opponents could sometimes be found in the government's courts. It was there that some progressive legislation was eventually eliminated, with judges declaring some acts to be unconstitutional. In 1905, for example, the United States Supreme Court struck down a New York State law that had limited the working hours of the state's bakery employees. In the decision *Lochner v. New York*, the Supreme Court ruled that the law "infringed on the right of the bakers under the Fourteenth Amendment to get the best reward for their labor."[61] Other decisions that stymied progressive laws included a 1908 decision that invalidated the Employers' Liabilities Act, which protected workers from unsafe working conditions and held employers liable. The court also decided to limit the power of a hatters union through its decision in *Loewe v. Lawlor*.

The courts did not always decide against progressive legislation, however. In 1908, the Supreme Court ruled in favor of Progressivism in the case *Muller v. Oregon*. The decision upheld an Oregon law that limited the number of hours that women could be employed. (Women were often hired and overworked by employers because they would accept lower wages than men.) Nevertheless, President Roosevelt had little appreciation for many of the decisions the Supreme Court made regarding the constitutionality of progressive legislation. He considered the Supreme Court to be an obstacle to these new laws.

Throughout his presidency, as Roosevelt supported Progressivism, the American public remained loyal. He was still so popular in 1908 that he was virtually able to handpick his successor as Republican president. He threw his support to his secretary of war, William Howard Taft. Taft was accepted by the party, nominated as the Republican candidate, and won the election, allowing the party to hold onto the White House for another four years. Although Taft would prove to be more tepid on Progressivism than Roosevelt, Americans had managed to elect yet one more national leader intent on continuing support for Progressivism.

8

Taft at the Helm

Increasingly throughout his presidency, Theodore Roosevelt had become a champion of at least a limited form of Progressivism. He had driven bills though Congress and, in many ways, set the progressive agenda for the country. Roosevelt had not simply served as president, he had taken command of the office and exerted more power and force of political will than perhaps any of his predecessors. Roosevelt *was* the presidency, and the office would never be the same. His two terms had ushered the presidency into the twentieth century, creating a modern executive branch. Many of his positions and directions received support from the majority of the American people, and Roosevelt left the White House as popular as he had entered it. To the public, Roosevelt was "the Trustbuster," a champion of the people as much as any Populist had ever been. He had granted his favor to William Howard Taft, who would then follow in his footsteps. Roosevelt's shoes often seemed too large for Taft, though. Not only the public, but also Roosevelt and even Taft himself, thought so.

THE RELUCTANT PRESIDENT

Despite having been virtually handed the presidency on a plate—Taft had defeated his Democratic opponent,

William Jennings Bryan, by 159 electoral votes—Taft was no Roosevelt. He had not even aspired to become president, wanting instead a nomination to the Supreme Court. In part, he had accepted the nomination only because his wife desperately wanted him to be president and for herself to be first lady. The contrasts between Taft and Roosevelt were sometimes stark. Roosevelt was extremely gregarious and outgoing to the point of being self-serving and obnoxious, whereas Taft was quieter, unaccustomed to the limelight. As one historian has described him, the new president was "good-natured, easygoing, grotesquely overweight."[62] He had less drive and ambition than Roosevelt, as well as less imagination. Taft also had little experience with party politics. Born in Cincinnati, Ohio, Taft became a lawyer and a federal judge. He then was selected as the American governor of the Philippines in 1900 after the United States gained the island nation from Spain after the Spanish-American War. In that role, he had proven himself a capable bureaucrat and administrator, and Roosevelt appointed him secretary of war. During this time, Taft had served as the coordinator of the building of the Panama Canal when Roosevelt handed control of the Central American construction project over to the U.S. Army. Taft became Roosevelt's right-hand man. When the president headed west on vacation and hunting expeditions, he would leave Taft to run things. As Roosevelt would describe to reporters, he was certain, in his absences, that Taft was "sitting on the lid" of the executive branch.[63] None of these roles had actually equipped Taft for the White House, though, and throughout his presidency, Taft seemed to struggle with self-doubt. He once related that "whenever someone said 'Mr. President,' he looked around for Roosevelt."[64]

Although William Howard Taft believed in such progressive policies as trust busting, he tended to be more conservative than his predecessor, which drew the ire of both Theodore Roosevelt and his Progressive allies. Taft is pictured here in 1911 speaking to a crowd at the Manassas Courthouse in Virginia.

Nevertheless, Taft earnestly approached his presidency with every intention of creating a legacy of his own even if it was based on little more than continuing Roosevelt's agendas. That was, after all, what Roosevelt expected of him. Roosevelt had met with some opposition on several of his progressive goals during the last two years in office. The 1908 election results included wins on behalf of several progressive Republicans, and Taft hoped that those new votes would help him pass bills that had become stuck in the process of becoming law.

TAKING UP THE TARIFF

Despite his plans and intentions, however, Taft soon faced difficult political problems. His party was technically split on the issues surrounding Progressivism. Republican conservatives who had given up on Roosevelt soft-pedaling change and reform hoped that Taft would cooperate with them in slowing the Progressive movement. Republican Party Progressives, however, wanted the new president to go even further than Roosevelt had in the reform arena. Several of the newly elected Republicans had campaigned by calling for more progressive reform. They had promised to revise tariffs, even though they had not specified whether tariffs should be increased or decreased. Tariffs would, indeed, become Taft's first order of business. The issue would not go well for the new chief executive.

When he tackled the tariff question, Taft was taking up an issue that Roosevelt had chosen to simply put off during both his terms in office. The more progressive Republicans wanted to see tariffs reduced, along with a general move away from the government's reliance on customs duties and protectionism. The more conservative Republicans favored tariffs, believing them to be an important part of their party's platform. They wanted to see tariffs increased because, theoretically, such tariffs protected American businesses. Taft was left in the middle to wade troubled political waters.

To try to gain the support of the majority of the Republicans in Congress, Taft gave his support to the reselection of a conservative Republican speaker of the House, Joseph G. Cannon, "an old and fervent enemy of tariff reforms."[65] The move was a daring one: If Taft were to stand up to the old-line speaker, Cannon could place innumerable roadblocks in the way of progressive legislation. When the congressional session opened in March 1909, the tariff issue took center stage. Taft requested that Congress pass a new tariff package that would largely lower tariff rates on most imports. The following month, the House of Representatives cooperated, passing a tariff bill that reduced rates on sugar, iron, and lumber while completely eliminating tariffs on coal and cattle hides. The true fight would be in the Senate, though: Of its 100 members, 61 were Republicans and 31 Democrats. Despite this majority, however, Senator Aldrich managed to antagonize several progressive Republicans, including Robert La Follette of Wisconsin and others who wanted lower tariffs. Aldrich was unable to block the Taft-supported tariff bill. Instead, he used his power to have 800 amendments written into the bill through the Senate Finance Committee, many of which actually raised tariffs on a variety of goods. His actions outraged La Follette and other Midwestern progressive senators throughout the summer of 1909.

This struggle would place President Taft awkwardly between both conservative and progressive Republicans. When the Aldrich-altered tariff bill finally passed in early July, by a vote of 45 to 34, congressmen looked to Taft for leadership. Although his original tariff bill had been largely gutted, Taft went along with the new tariff legislation and signed the Payne-Aldrich Tariff in August. Only conservative Republicans were happy with the outcome. Progressives within his own party were angry with Taft for having given in on the tariff issue. Then, when Taft did not support the appointment of several candidates that progressive Republicans suggested for federal positions, Taft lost further ground with them.

CONSERVATION BATTLE

Taft was quickly losing ground within his own party. Early the following year, another conflict further damaged Taft's reputation with Progressives and even with Theodore Roosevelt himself. (When Taft took office, Roosevelt was out of the country, having gone to Africa on an extended hunting

Unlike his predecessor, William Taft was not a conservationist and openly clashed with Gifford Pinchot (pictured here), the first chief of the U.S. Forest Service. Taft removed Pinchot from his post in 1910 after Pinchot openly criticized the president for opening federal lands in Alaska for settlement.

safari.) In early 1910, Taft clashed with a leftover Roosevelt appointee. Gifford Pinchot was the nation's chief forester and one of Roosevelt's leading advocates of conservation. Taft and Pinchot did not like one another. Taft had privately questioned some of Roosevelt's conservation measures when Roosevelt was president, thinking them to be beyond the scope and power of the presidency. Working with his secretary of the Interior, Richard A. Ballinger, Taft allowed for the opening of some western federal lands in Alaska for private development, lands that Pinchot had closed off to settlement and exploitation. When a Land Office investigator, Louis R. Glavis, realized that the land had been opened, he turned the information over to Pinchot.

Glavis and Pinchot then collaborated on some "muckraking" articles for *Collier's* magazine (Glavis had been fired by Taft by then) and the public became indignant at Ballinger's actions. Taft sided with Ballinger. An angry Pinchot wrote a letter to a senator to complain about the situation, a letter that was soon released to the press, and President Taft removed Pinchot from his post for insubordination. Still in Africa, Roosevelt received word of the firing and was immediately angry and disappointed in Taft. Perhaps, he had erred in supporting Taft for the presidency. Taft had not yet been president for a year, and already Roosevelt was considering a run against him for the presidency in 1912.

In the aftermath of the Pinchot affair, Progressives in Congress sided with the fired chief forester and called for a special House-Senate investigation to look into the Alaskan land question. Neither Ballinger nor Taft was found guilty of anything, but the separation between the president and the Progressives was widened in the process.

Other problems for Taft came up that spring, when progressive Republicans banded with Democrats against Speaker of the House Cannon. Cannon often stood in the way of important progressive legislation. Because Taft had supported Aldrich during the tariff debate, the move was taken as a slap against the president. It was not that all progressive bills were stymied in Congress—by 1910, measures such as railroad legislation designed to strengthen the Interstate Commerce Commission were passed, along with a progressive law designed to support private citizens who used federal banks located in the nation's post offices— but even as such laws were created, Taft was receiving virtually no credit for them. In fact, Progressives claimed that President Taft often hampered such reform.

Then, the congressional elections of 1910 sent a startling message to President Taft. That fall, many Republican candidates stumped against the tariff that had been passed and against those whom they considered responsible for it, including Speaker Cannon, Senator Aldrich, and President Taft. Progressive Republicans won one primary after another, defeating 41 congressional incumbents. When the election was held, additional Republican conservatives lost to Democratic candidates. When the smoke cleared, the Democrats had wrested control of the House of Representatives. The Senate fell under the control of a combination of Democrats and progressive Republicans.

PROGRESSIVE INROADS

During the second half of Taft's single term as president, moves on behalf of Progressivism increased as Congress gave the movement its general support. The will of Congress mirrored that of the American public, it seemed, and conservatives in both parties found themselves sometimes ducking for cover as the reformers set out to bring about change. It was not done without some level of involvement from Taft, however. Although Taft was more conservative than Roosevelt, he was not opposed to some progressive measures. He had his own reform agenda. Regarding big business, Taft proved to be more of a "trustbuster" than Roosevelt: the U.S. Justice Department filed "twice as many antitrust suits in four years as Roosevelt had in seven."[66] Ironically, one of those antitrust suits would bring Roosevelt out publicly against President Taft.

WOMEN ON THE MARCH

The direction of the Progressive movement between 1910 and 1913 was sometimes set by neither political party nor the president. In the spring of 1910, the National American Woman Suffrage Association (NAWSA) delivered a petition to Congress, a grassroots document that bore 400,000 signatures in support of a constitutional amendment that would grant the vote to women across the country. It was not the first serious women's rights effort in American history: More than 50 years earlier, women's advocates such as Lucretia Coffin Mott, Elizabeth Cady Stanton, and Susan B. Anthony had written and rallied on behalf of women's rights. After two generations of campaigning through the second half of the 1800s, however, only four states had passed legislation to grant women the right to vote.

Within the mood of Progressivism as it stood in 1910, the women's suffrage movement was gaining new ground. Women across the country were participating in rallies, speaking out for themselves, and delivering large petitions to Congress in numbers as never seen before. The symbolic color for the suffragettes was yellow, and many made a practice of wearing flowers such as yellow daisies, buttercups, and jonquils. Groups such as the Political Equality Association, established by one of the leading society women of New York, Mrs. O.H.P. Belmont, organized many of the political efforts to support the vote for women. Famous people, including political figures, artists, and actresses such as Lillian Russell, joined the crusade. An earlier generation of women's rights advocates had stumped with little impact, but by the first decade of the twentieth century, as one suffragette noted, the cause of liberating women "is actually fashionable now."[67]

Women were marching everywhere it seemed. A month after delivering their petition to Congress, on a rainy May day, a march was held along New York City's Fifth Avenue, where "an unlikely army of hobble-skirted matrons and bright-eyed young girls"[68] clamored for the vote as they carried banners that read "I Wish Ma Could Vote" along with American flags. Two years later, another march that drew 15,000 suffragettes who were cheered on by a street crowd that numbered half a million, took place on Fifth Avenue. Three years later, another Fifth Avenue march involved 40,000 supporters, including the Men's League for Woman Suffrage. There were marches from coast to coast, including Seattle and Washington, D.C., where a 1914 rally

In the spring of 1910, the National American Woman Suffrage Association (NAWSA) presented a petition to Congress that contained 400,000 signatures in support of a constitutional amendment granting women the right to vote. Here, members of the group march in a suffragette parade in New York City in May 1913.

included "10 bands, 50 women on horseback, and platoons of government dignitaries."[69]

Slowly but steadily, the vote was granted to American women. The movement relied on female leadership, including that of Alice Paul. Other leaders included Lucy Burns and Harriet Stanton Blatch, the daughter of nineteenth-century women's rights leader Elizabeth Cady Stanton. Progress was made along the way. Some states— including Wyoming (1890), Colorado (1893), and Utah and Idaho (1896)—had already voted to allow women to vote in national elections. Additional states, including Washington (1910), California (1911), and Arizona, Oregon, and Kansas (1912), also passed laws to grant female suffrage. Similar laws failed in Ohio, Wisconsin, and Michigan.

Ironically, perhaps, Progressives were not always supportive of the women's rights movement of the early twentieth century. President Roosevelt referred to himself as a less than "enthusiastic advocate" of the cause. "I do not think giving the women suffrage," he stated, "will produce any marked improvement in the condition for women."[70] Woodrow Wilson, elected to the presidency in 1912 at the height of the movement, did not lend his support to the vote for women until 1918. By then, the campaign had nearly won its goal.

Finally, on June 4, 1919, the campaign triumphed. On that date, Congress passed the Nineteenth Amendment to the U.S. Constitution, which stated that no American citizen could be denied the vote "on account of sex."[71] Suddenly, more than 25 million women could vote. The scope of the progressive change was immense. "The victory is not a victory for women alone," noted the *Kansas City Star*, "it is a victory for democracy and the principle of equality upon which the nation was founded."[72]

ROOSEVELT AND HIS NEW NATIONALISM

Progressives found the administration of President Taft to be a disappointment overall, and former President Theodore Roosevelt was even more disgruntled with the man he had chosen to succeed him as chief executive. As early as 1910, before the elections, Roosevelt was back in the country from his extended safari in Africa. He did not wait long to bring himself back into the political arena. In a speech delivered in Osawatomie, Kansas, during the 1910 campaigns, he spoke of the need for greater responsibility on the part of the federal government to rein in big business and give support to laborers and others. He gave his agenda a name: New Nationalism.

Largely, Roosevelt kept his public animosity and disappointment about Taft to a minimum until the fall of 1911. He was angered when Taft ordered his attorney general to file an antitrust suit against United States Steel, which was then owned by J. Pierpont Morgan. Roosevelt and Morgan had made certain agreements that the president would not file such a suit against U.S. Steel because Morgan had helped stabilize the American economy during the Panic of 1907. Now it seemed that all bets were off and Taft was proceeding against the giant steel company. Roosevelt took the decision personally. Soon, he was speaking publicly against Taft. By early 1912, Progressives were approaching Roosevelt about running for reelection. Along with them were several Republican Party regulars who were also disappointed with Taft. By February 21, Roosevelt had made his decision: He would run again for president. In making his announcement, he coined a new phrase: "My hat is in the ring," to which he added, "The fight is on and I'm stripped to the buff!"[73]

Roosevelt began to tout his progressive agenda, speaking publicly in support of more legislation and in favor of the referendum and the recall. Such statements went well with Progressives but were not popular with conservatives, especially within Roosevelt's party, the Republicans. Despite his rhetoric and his general popularity with the

TARGETING THEODORE

The presidential election of 1912 was an exciting race as three of the nation's most popular and well-known politicians campaigned for the office. One surprising event was an assassination attempt on one of the candidates, Theodore Roosevelt, in Milwaukee.

Roosevelt was in the Wisconsin city to attend a political rally at which he would deliver a speech. He did not know that he had been stalked for several weeks by a New York saloonkeeper named John Schrank. Then in his mid-30s, Schrank had immigrated to the United States at age 13, had lost his parents while still young, and had inherited valuable New York properties from an uncle who raised him. As a young man, Schrank sold his lands and took up a life with little direction. He often wandered the streets of New York at night and was known for being highly religious.

It is unclear exactly why Schrank targeted Roosevelt for assassination, but it appears that he had become mentally unbalanced and was obsessed with Roosevelt's serving three times as president, thinking no one should serve three terms. (Never mind that Roosevelt had inherited the presidency after William McKinley's assassination and had been elected to the White House only once, in 1904.) In September 1912, Schrank even claimed to have been visited by McKinley's ghost. The former president's spirit asked Schrank to avenge his death, implying that Roosevelt was responsible.

That fall, Schrank began to follow Roosevelt from city to city, looking for an opportunity to shoot the former president. Finally, he found his opportunity in Milwaukee.

American people, Roosevelt would not succeed in locking in the Republican Party nomination. Taft himself came out swinging, giving a bitter speech in April in which he said, "Condemn me if you will, but condemn me by other witnesses than Theodore Roosevelt. I was a man of straw; but I have been a man of straw long enough."[74] By the time

On the evening of October 14, after waiting outside the Hotel Gilpatrick, where Roosevelt was staying, he approached his target on the street and fired a single shot from a handgun.

Schrank's .32-caliber bullet struck Roosevelt in the chest, where it lodged. The wound might have been more severe, but the projectile had passed first through a metal eyeglass case in Roosevelt's coat pocket, as well as a double-folded copy of his 50-page speech. The former president was also wearing a heavy overcoat, which slowed the bullet. Once struck, Roosevelt refused to go to the hospital and went to the hall to deliver his bullet-scarred speech. He opened his political address by informing the audience of his wound: "I don't know whether you fully understand that I have just been shot; but it takes more than that to kill a Bull Moose!"* He spoke for 90 minutes. After his address, Roosevelt finally went to a local hospital. After examining the wound, doctors decided that it would be riskier to remove the bullet than to leave it in Roosevelt's chest, so it remained in Roosevelt. He carried it for the rest of his life.

Schrank was eventually found to be insane and spent the remaining 31 years of his life in the Central State Mental Hospital in Waupun, Wisconsin. He lived until 1943. Three years earlier, Theodore Roosevelt's distant cousin Franklin Roosevelt had been elected to a third term as president. A year after Schrank's death, the second Roosevelt was elected to a fourth term.

---

* "John F. Schrank." Wikipedia.org. Available online at *http://en.wikipedia.org/wiki/John_Schrank*.

of the Republican Convention in Chicago in June, Taft supporters had control of the convention and renominated their standard bearer, President Taft. Not to be left behind, by August, Roosevelt, along with Robert La Follette, had broken from party ranks and formed the Progressive Party, which nominated Roosevelt for the presidency. The new political party was able to attract supporters from both the Republican and Democratic parties, as well as from progressive reformers across the country.

It was a progressive heyday. Every candidate supported some level of Progressivism. When the Democrats nominated a moderate reform candidate, New Jersey governor Woodrow Wilson, they built their party platform on favoring collective bargaining for labor unions, changes in the nation's banking system, and the abolition of giant corporations (instead of regulating them). Candidate Wilson even had a label for his party's proposed progressive platform: New Freedom. Roosevelt and the Progressives supported the prohibition of child labor, minimum wages for women workers, workmen's compensation, and banking and currency reform. Even the more conservative Republicans who backed Taft supported a variety of moderate reform measures, including more regulation of trusts and banking reform. These progressive positions were eclipsed by the radicalism of a fourth candidate, Eugene V. Debs, a Socialist whose party called for government ownership of all of the nation's resources and industry.

When the vote was taken in November, the Republicans were woefully split. Roosevelt received 4.1 million votes to Taft's 3.5 million. Wilson garnered 6.3 million, giving him a plurality over his challengers. Obviously, the combined vote for Roosevelt and Taft totaled more than Wilson's numbers, but the die was cast: Roosevelt had split the party, ensuring a Democratic win. (Debs did receive one million votes. He was serving a term in prison at the time.) A Democrat would soon occupy the White House. With only one exception—President Cleveland, who was elected both in 1884 and 1892—it was the first time the Democrats had won the presidency since James Buchanan's election in 1856.

Wilson in the White House

Newly elected President Woodrow Wilson came into the White House under circumstances previous presidents would have envied. Democrats held majorities in both houses of Congress, and "if there were conservatives among the Democrats, there were plenty of progressive Republicans to offset them."[75] He would have solid support from the new congressmen, who accounted for 40 percent of congressional Democrats. They did not have a track record in Congress and would be ready to gain points with the new president. Wilson could expect to wield his presidential power with few restrictions, except those required by the Constitution. The election proved that the American people wanted to see more Progressivism practiced by the White House. Wilson was only too willing to serve that public interest. He would prove to be a capable, intelligent, and extremely articulate national leader. He did, however, experience several small strokes before his inauguration that seem to have hardened him to unsolicited advice and criticism, as well as to have increased his stubborn nature.

WILSON CHAMPIONS THE CAUSE

As soon as he entered office, Wilson began pushing his progressive policies. In his inaugural address, the new chief executive spoke out against the destructive elements of industrialism. He requested that the new Congress take up the issue of tariff reform. To emphasize his message, in April 1913, just weeks after taking office, Wilson spoke directly to Congress, delivering a formal message. No president had addressed Congress that way since Thomas Jefferson in 1801. In his speech, Wilson asked the House and Senate to reduce import tariffs. Indeed, the Democrat-controlled Congress did just that. The Underwood Tariff (Congressman Oscar W. Underwood was the chair of the House Ways and Means Committee, one of the legislature's more powerful committees) cut import tariffs on wool, sugar, cotton products, and silks. To make up for the loss of national income, Congress included a small tax on incomes of the wealthy, those who made more than $4,000 per year. The rates were higher on those who earned more than $20,000 annually. Through its progressive actions, Congress soon secured ratification of the Sixteenth Amendment to the United States Constitution, which created an income tax, a progressive measure.

Although the bill passed the House, congressmen were uncertain that it would make its way through the Senate. They had seen earlier tariff fights in 1894 and 1909. In contrast to these earlier examples, however, the Senate of 1913, dominated by Democrats, was fairly united and the new tariff bill was passed in August by a vote of 44 to 37. Wilson placed his signature on the bill in October, giving the new president and his Democrat supporters in Congress a singular progressive victory.

PROGRESS FOR THE BANKS

With this early success, Wilson soon took on another progressive idea, one he had campaigned on during the election. Most of the country's political leaders recognized the need for banking reform. As the Panic of 1907 revealed, the U.S. economy in the early years of the twentieth century could not reasonably function without the existence of a centralized banking system with enough power to "control the currency, meet the monetary needs of different sections of the country, and ensure that the money supply was adequate to the demands of the growing economy."[76]

The answer to this national economic problem had been proposed even before Wilson was elected in 1912. With Nelson Aldrich leading the way, the National Monetary Commission had suggested that private bankers should be responsible for supervising a system of reserve banks. Wilson had supported the idea, but, once he became president, his newly appointed secretary of state, William Jennings Bryan, and supporters in Congress suggested that the federal government would need to maintain control and jurisdiction over any reserve banks that might be established under any new political agreement. Wilson would come to agree with Bryan's proposal.

Wilson and his supporters in Congress were able to facilitate getting a banking bill through Congress within six months. Wilson had to appease several groups, including Southern and Western Democrats in his party. These groups wanted to see an expansion of credit to farmers, as well as an end to the practice of "interlocking directorates," which allowed bankers to serve as directors of banks that they otherwise competed against. The new banking bill was greatly supported by Wilson, who took many hits from the banking community as he called in favors and used his powers of persuasion to gain support from Senate Democrats who first opposed him on this issue. Once again, President Wilson was able to coordinate efforts to bring about significant progressive legislation during his first year in office, signing the bill to create the Federal Reserve System on December 27. It would prove to be one of the most

In 1912, Democrat Woodrow Wilson was elected the twenty-eighth president of the United States. Wilson (*third from left*) defeated both incumbent William Howard Taft and former president Theodore Roosevelt, who was the Progressive Party candidate.

important congressional acts of the first half of the twentieth century. The new act established the Federal Reserve Board, with the president appointing its members. A national system of 12 regional banking districts was established across the country. The Federal Reserve was empowered to place money in circulation, to expand or contract credit as the nation's economy dictated, and to try to stave off the extremes of the national economic cycle that had, for more than a century, alternately created solid, positive economic times and crushing downturns. Throughout the twentieth century, the Federal Reserve worked to balance the national economy, with mixed results. Within less than a generation of the creation of the Federal Reserve, the United States experienced its worst depression to date.

WILSON FURTHERS HIS PROGRESSIVE AGENDA

With these early successes on behalf of Progressivism, Wilson had made great strides in support of the need for reform and progress. He had fulfilled his campaign promise to reduce the tariff, taken control of America's business trusts, and improved the nation's banking system. He had taken on, in a meaningful way, those parts of the U.S. economy that he referred to as the "triple wall of privilege"—tariffs, banking, and trusts.[77] By early 1914, he once again took his message to Congress and the American people, requesting additional legislation regarding business trusts. Many congressmen continued to give the president their support and, before the end of 1914, Wilson and Congress had put together and passed the Clayton Antitrust Act. Its purpose was to "spell out precisely the business practices that restricted competition and then prohibit them."[78] The act made several previous business practices, such as price discrimination, which gave large businesses an advantage over small businesses, and the existence of "holding companies," which were sometimes nothing more than trusts dressed up in a thin disguise, illegal.

The Clayton Antitrust Act was a favorite of America's labor unionists. One of its ramifications was to declare strikes to be legal under federal law, sanctioning the use of the main weapons of the nation's workers—the strike, the picket, and the boycott. The act also omitted labor unions from prosecution in cases based on antitrust laws. Some of America's most important labor leaders, including

Samuel Gompers, gave their enthusiastic support to the Clayton Act.

The year 1914 also saw passage of an act that created the Federal Trade Commission (FTC); its purpose was to take a hands-on role in directing and overseeing the country's business activity. The trade commission was not a new idea. Theodore Roosevelt had proposed something similar in 1912 during the presidential campaign. The commission was empowered to review any proposed mergers of large corporations and to make rulings on the legality or constitutionality of business methods and transactions or the formation of business combinations. The FTC would continue to wield power throughout the twentieth century.

WILSON'S FAILURES

Such progressive measures won the hearts of many reformers in the United States, but Wilson would also disappoint them sometimes. After creating the FTC, Wilson gave some indications that he thought his progressive agenda had been largely put in place and that little was left to do. Progressives were not satisfied with that attitude, believing that Wilson needed to push harder to bring about social change through legislation. One of the most important changes Progressives wanted to make was concerned with racial equality. The years of the early twentieth century were notorious for the general treatment of blacks and other racial groups, who were often discriminated against and mistreated because the law did not specifically or consistently protect them. Between 1900 and 1915, more than 1,000 blacks, mostly men, were killed by being hanged (the word used at the time was "lynched"), burned, or shot. Eight million black citizens lived in Southern states, where they were subject to the restrictions of "Jim Crow" laws, which authorized segregation to keep the races apart in everything from using the same public facilities to whether they were allowed to receive an education. Wilson had no desire to support such race-based federal laws to protect blacks. He did not think that the national government needed to play an important role in such issues and that new policies based on new laws might upset the balance between blacks and whites.

Wilson, a Southerner by birth, was something of a racist himself. In fact, his administration took steps to encourage and expand racial segregation throughout the federal government. When Wilson's postmaster general, Albert S. Burleson, made a suggestion during an April 1913 cabinet meeting that black federal employees should be segregated from white workers, Wilson gave his support. Black workers soon discovered that they had to eat in separate lunchrooms from whites, as well as use separate restroom facilities. When black leaders, including those in the National Association for the Advancement of Colored People (NAACP) protested, Wilson seemed surprised. "I honestly believe segregation to be in the best interest of the colored people," the president stated, "as exempting them from friction and criticism."[79]

ADDITIONAL PROGRESSIVE MEASURES

Although Wilson gave some indications in 1914 that much of the progressive agenda had been enacted, there would be additional measures passed even before the end of his first term as president. In the spring of 1916, Congress, with Wilson's blessing, passed the Adamson Act, which provided for an eight-hour day for all workers in interstate commerce. This affected thousands of railroad workers, as well as many others. Before that year was over, other acts were passed as well. The Kern-McGillicuddy Act established a model workmen's compensation program, but it applied only to federal employees. The Keating-Owen Act of 1916 banned the shipment across state lines of goods and products manufactured by child workers under the age of 14. (Two years later, this act was declared unconstitutional by the U.S. Supreme Court.) These successes in the name of Progressivism pushed the agenda of the movement even further.

The year 1916 marked something of an end to this steady stream of new congressional acts centered on progressive reform. By then, President Wilson and many Americans focused on the developing conflict in Europe that came to be known as World War I. Much of the nation's energy and spirit was spent on this large-scale international conflict. In many ways, the progressive drive was rerouted from the progressive agenda to another pair of goals—supporting the Allies against Germany and others and then joining the war by sending American troops to European battlefields. In either case, Americans were reluctant to criticize their country in the midst of a global conflict.

Because the war took precedence over most proposals concerned with social and economic reform, the Progressive movement took serious hits during the conflict that would include the United States as a direct combatant nation by the spring of 1917. Not all issues that concerned Progressivism would be shelved during the war, however: The women's suffrage movement did not give up its call for the female vote in 1917 or 1918. The war itself, in fact, gave greater purpose and justification to the campaign. With so many men off to war, women were giving support in every way possible. They filled the ranks of industrial workers, producing everything from tanks to planes, and served as nurses and volunteers by the hundreds of thousands. Even Wilson, who had been tepid concerning the female vote previously, finally spoke in favor of the suffrage movement in 1918. The war would

THE TWENTIETH-CENTURY MARCH OF PROGRESSIVISM

By the end of the second decade of the 1900s, those who supported Progressivism began to take account of the changes that they had helped bring about during the previous 20 years. In the postwar era of the 1920s, the movement seemed to fragment, and little progressive legislation or social change was made. In the end, the reach of the Progressive movement of the early twentieth century exceeded its grasp. The vision of its supporters and advocates would not become a complete reality, although the movement did manage to make strides on behalf of a greater level of democratic practice in America and an expanded role for government as an agent of positive change.

Progressivism appeared to have run its course by 1920, but the call for political and social reform in the United States would not die. Government was different because of the movement. There were other reforms yet to take place, and many would have their day in the decades that followed. By the 1930s, when devastating depression sank the country into a dark hole of economic downturn, people would look to the government to solve their latest problems. Another Roosevelt, Franklin Delano, would lead the country through the decade, using the power of the federal government to create regulatory agencies, provide direct and indirect relief to Americans, retool the business and commercial worlds to provide stability and growth,

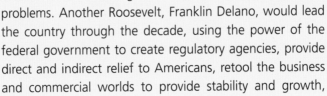

end before the ratification of a constitutional amendment in support of suffrage, but it would become law in 1920, in time to allow women to vote for a new president that November.

Another reform movement also peaked during the years of the Great War. The drive to bring about Prohibition, a national ban on alcohol, had been under way since the early twentieth century. Earlier attempts to limit America's alcohol consumption habits had taken place during the 1830s and 1840s and had resulted in prohibition laws being passed in and otherwise use the power of the republic to steer through the difficult waters of the Great Depression.

During the 1950s and 1960s, another form of Progressivism took root, giving voice to the civil rights movement and the reach of President Lyndon Johnson's Great Society, which was represented by a raft of social and economic reforms established by the federal government to expand voting rights, government housing, welfare, education, and Medicare. Johnson's social programs could make the claim that the government was pursuing a greater progressive agenda than that established between 1900 and 1920.

In the past 40 years, progressive legislation has not been abandoned. During the 1970s, in the midst of the scandal that would bring down President Richard Nixon, the "muckraking" spirit was embodied in the investigative journalism that sought answers to the larger questions of Watergate and the misuse of government power. During the 1980s, perhaps, the progressive agenda took a back seat to ending the cold war, but America and its government had changed much by the latter years of the twentieth century through the continuing spirit of Progressivism. Today, as social injustice, racial discrimination, and economic challenges raise their heads in America, Progressivism remains the nation's most viable alternative to righting its wrongs.

Maine in 1851. Similar laws were created throughout the remainder of the 1800s. By 1900, one-fourth of Americans lived in communities where drinking or saloons and taverns were limited or banned altogether. With the arrival of the new century, various groups—including the Woman's Christian Temperance Union, the Anti-Saloon League, and the Methodist Church—were joining forces against what they considered the evils of alcohol. This movement succeeded where earlier movements had failed for several reasons: The Progressives were able to use the influence they had with various legislatures. The problem had grown to considerable proportions by then, with annual beer consumption in the United States having risen from 36 million gallons in 1850 to more than 850 million gallons by 1890, a massive increase even considering that the population during those 40 years had tripled. Sometimes the temperance supporters blamed the increase on the large number of Irish, Italian, and German immigrants to the United States, but this hardly served as an explanation. This new campaign in favor of temperance helped create "dry" laws in two of every three states and, by World War

One of the Progressive Party's key reforms was the passage of the Eighteenth Amendment, which banned the consumption, distribution, production, and sale of alcohol. Here, more than 33,000 gallons of wine are pumped into a Los Angeles sewer during prohibition.

I, 75 percent of Americans lived in places where they could not legally purchase alcohol, including beer.

The war itself was another incentive to further action. Critics of America's addiction to heavy drink argued that, every time grain was used to produce alcohol, it denied food to someone who was starving in Europe because of the war. On December 18, 1917 (the year America entered World War I), Congress passed the Eighteenth Amendment to the Constitution, banning the production, sale, distribution, and consumption of alcohol. On January 29, 1919, the amendment was finally ratified, becoming the law of a dry and sober land, although the amendment did not go into effect for another year. Prohibition, yet another piece of legislation brought about by the Progressive movement, would remain in effect until 1933.

Some supporters of the Progressive movement assumed that, once the war ended, the United States would return to the drawing board of reform and give its support to additional measures to improve the lives of even more Americans and to help create more support for the country's downtrodden. It was not to be. After years of criticism and campaigns that focused on the country's problems and shortcomings, postwar Americans were largely tired of the movement. The war increased the desire among many people to return to simpler times, to move away from international conflicts and the constant shirttail tug of America's nagging problems.

For a while, Progressivism had spent much of its energy on righting America's wrongs and repairing its faults. The Progressive movement had had its day, and America was a better place already, many thought. After the war, Americans wanted to experience a good time, longing to revel in the promise of a new decade. This national desire was described by the Republican candidate for the presidency in 1920, Warren Gamaliel Harding, who called for the country to

"Return to Normalcy," to a time when the United States was less world weary and more innocent, reliant on remaining out from under the influence of international rivalries and conflicts. America's problems would not disappear in the new decade of the Roaring Twenties, but further reforms and a revival of the spirit of the Progressives would have to wait for another opportunity to bring about change in an imperfect America.

CHRONOLOGY

1890   The Sherman Antitrust Act is passed by Congress.

1892   Farmers form a third political party called the People's Party, otherwise known as the Populists; they support James B. Weaver as their reform candidate for president.

1894   An urban reform group, the National Municipal League, is established.

1896   Populists and Democrats join forces in support of Populist candidates, including Nebraskan William Jennings Bryan for president.

1897   Progressive Samuel Jones is elected mayor of Toledo; he is reelected several times and dies in office in 1904.

1900   Progressive reformer Robert La Follette is elected governor of Wisconsin; as governor, La Follette supports reforms such as the direct primary and a railroad tax bill.

1901   Republican President William McKinley is assassinated, making his vice president, Theodore Roosevelt, president; Roosevelt orders the Justice Department to file an antitrust suit against Northern Securities.

1902   La Follette is reelected governor of Wisconsin and continues his progressive agenda; *McClure's* magazine runs a series on city corruption written by Lincoln Steffens; President Roosevelt pushes the Newlands Act through Congress.

1902–1903   Muckraker Ida Tarbell publishes her exposé on John Rockefeller and Standard Oil.

1903   President Roosevelt convinces Congress to pass progressive legislation, including the Elkins Act and the Expedition Act; he creates his first federal bird sanctuary at Pelican Island, Florida.

1904   La Follette is elected to a third term as Wisconsin governor; that year, the U.S. Supreme Court orders the Northern Securities trust to be broken up and Roosevelt is elected president.

1905   The U.S. Supreme Court strikes down a New York law that would limit the working hours of the state's bakers (*Lochner v. New York*).

1906   La Follette is elected to the U.S. Senate; that year, Theodore Roosevelt uses the term *muckraker* to refer to Progressive writers; writer Upton

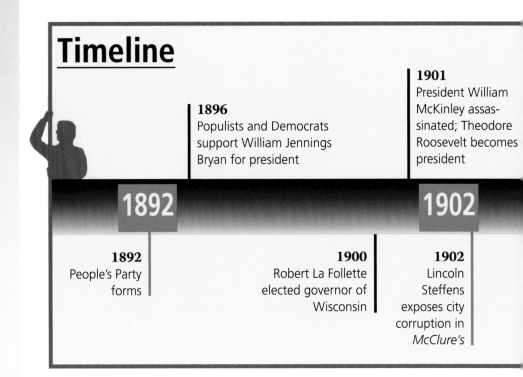

Timeline

1896
Populists and Democrats support William Jennings Bryan for president

1901
President William McKinley assassinated; Theodore Roosevelt becomes president

1892

1902

1892
People's Party forms

1900
Robert La Follette elected governor of Wisconsin

1902
Lincoln Steffens exposes city corruption in *McClure's*

Sinclair publishes his novel *The Jungle*, which is an exposé of the meatpacking industry; before year's end, Congress passes the Pure Food and Drug Act, as well as the Antiquities Act.

1907   Roosevelt withdraws millions of acres of federal land from private exploitation.

1907–1909   President Roosevelt supports legislation in Congress to create federal income taxes, the eight-hour workday, and the licensing of American corporations engaged in interstate commerce.

1908   U.S. Supreme Court decides *Muller v. Oregon* in support of an Oregon law that limited the number of working hours for women; William Howard Taft is elected president of the United States.

1902–1903
Ida Tarbell publishes exposé on Standard Oil

1904
U.S. Supreme Court breaks Northern Securities trust

1907
President Roosevelt withdraws millions of acres of federal land from private exploitation

1902

1907

1903
Progressive legislation passed, including the Elkins Act

1906
Pure Food and Drug Act and Antiquities Act passed

1910   President Taft fires chief forester Gifford Pinchot, one of Roosevelt's appointees; a storm of controversy follows, drawing in Roosevelt; The National American Woman Suffrage Association hands Congress a petition signed by 400,000 individuals calling for a women's vote amendment to the Constitution.

1911   The Triangle Shirtwaist Company fire claims 150 victims; the disaster leads to several Progressive measures.

1912   Democrat Woodrow Wilson is elected president.

1913   Congress creates the Federal Reserve System.

1914   More than 400 American cities have installed the independent commission form or municipal

1908
William
Howard Taft
elected
president

1911
Triangle
Shirtwaist
Company
fire claims
150 victims

1912
Woodrow
Wilson
elected
president

1907

1912

1907–1909
Legislation for federal income taxes, eight-hour workday, and licensing of American corporations engaged in interstate commerce proposed by President Roosevelt

1910
National American Woman Suffrage Association calls for a women's vote amendment to the Constitution

government; that year, Congress passes the Clayton Antitrust Act; Act that creates the Federal Trade Commission is passed.

1916   President Wilson supports passage of the Adamson Act, which sets an eight-hour workday for those who work in interstate commerce; Passage of Progressive bills such as the Kern-McGillicuddy Act and the Keating-Owen Act.

1917   The United States enters World War I, distracting many Americans from the causes of Progress-ivism; that year, Congress passes the Eighteenth Amendment to the Constitution, banning the sale and distribution of alcoholic drink.

1917
Congress
passes the
Eighteenth
Amendment
to the
Constitution

1920
States ratify
the proposed
amendment to
allow women
to vote

1913
Congress creates
the Federal
Reserve System

1913

1920

1916
President Wilson
supports passage of
the Adamson Act

1919
Congress passes
the Nineteenth
Amendment

1919   Congress passes the Nineteenth Amendment, which allows women to vote; the Eighteenth Amendment is finally ratified by the states.

1920   States ratify the proposed amendment to allow women to vote.

NOTES

CHAPTER 1

1. Allen Weinstein and R. Jackson Wilson, *Freedom and Crisis: An American History* (New York: Random House, 1974), 552.
2. Ibid.
3. Ibid.
4. Ibid., 553.
5. Ibid., 554.
6. Ibid., 555.
7. Ibid.
8. Ibid.
9. Ibid., 557.

CHAPTER 2

10. Time-Life Books, *Prelude to the Century* (Alexandria, Va.: Time-Life Books, 1998), 24.
11. Ibid., 26.
12. Fon W. Boardman, Jr., *America and the Progressive Era, 1900–1917* (New York: Henry Z. Walck, 1970), 49.
13. Ernest R. May, *The Progressive Era*, vol. 9, *1901–1917* (New York: Time Incorporated, 1964).
14. Time-Life, *Prelude to the Century*, 154.
15. Ibid.
16. Robert G. Athearn, *American Heritage Illustrated History of the United States*, vol. 11, *The Gilded Age* (New York: Choice Publishing, 1988), 932.

17. Time-Life, *Prelude to the Century*, 154.
18. Ibid., 156.
19. Ibid., 164.
20. Frederick Lewis Allen, *The Big Change: America Transforms Itself, 1900–1950* (New York: Harper & Brothers, 1952), 3.

CHAPTER 3

21. May, *Progressive Era*, 33.
22. Ibid.
23. Edward L. Ayers, *American Passages: A History of the United States* (Belmont, Calif.: Thomson Wadsworth, 2007), 507.
24. Ibid.
25. Ibid., 529
26. Ibid.
27. Ibid.
28. Allen, *The Big Change*, 57.
29. Ibid.
30. Ayers, *American Passages*, 530.
31. Ibid., 531.
32. Ibid.

CHAPTER 4

33. Robert G. Athearn, *American Heritage Illustrated History of the United States*, vol. 10, *The Age of Steel* (New York: Choice Publishing, 1988), 854.

34. Ayers, *American Passages*, 554.

35. May, *Progressive Era*, 53.

36. Ibid., 54.

CHAPTER 5

37. Ibid.

38. Ibid.

39. Ibid., 55.

40. Ayers, *American Passages*, 592.

41. May, *Progressive Era*, 56.

42. Ibid.

43. Ibid.

44. Ibid., 57.

45. Ibid., 58.

CHAPTER 6

46. Allen, *The Big Change*, 95.

47. May, *Progressive Era*, 72.

48. Ibid., 73.

49. Robert A. Rosenbaum, *The Penguin Encyclopedia of American History* (New York: Penguin Group, 2003), 347.

50. Allen, *The Big Change*, 96.

51. May, *Progressive Era*, 73.

52. Allen, *The Big Change*, 96.

53. May, *Progressive Era*, 73.

54. Allen, *The Big Change*, 96.

55. Ayers, *American Passages*, 585.

56. May, *Progressive Era*, 75.

57. Ibid.

CHAPTER 7

58. Ibid., 76.

59. Ibid., 77.

60. Ayers, *American Passages*, 595.

61. Ibid., 598.

CHAPTER 8

62. Ibid., 95.

63. Ayers, *American Passages*, 612.

64. May, *Progressive Era*, 95.

65. Ibid.

66. Ibid., 98.

67. Ayers, *American Passages*, 615.

68. Time-Life Books, *End of Innocence: 1910–1920* (Alexandria, Va.: Time-Life Books, 1998), 44.

69. Ibid., 49.

70. Michael V. Uschan, *A Cultural History of the United States: The 1910s* (San Diego, Calif.: Lucent Books, 1999), 34.

71. Time-Life, *End of Innocence*, 50.

72. Ibid.

73. Page Smith, *America Enters the World: A People's History of the Progressive Era and World War I* (New York: McGraw-Hill, 1985), 302.

74. May, *Progressive Era*, 99.

CHAPTER 9

75. Ibid., 101.

76. Ayers, *American Passages*, 627.

77. Thomas A. Bailey, *The American Pageant*, 5th ed., vol. II (Lexington, Mass.: D. C. Heath, 1975), 732.

78. Ayers, *American Passages*, 627.

79. Julie Jeffrey and Roy Jeffrey, eds. *The American People: Creating a Nation and Society*, 2nd ed. (New York: HarperCollins, 1990), 727.

BIBLIOGRAPHY

Allen, Frederick Lewis. *The Big Change: America Transforms Itself, 1900–1950*. New York: Harper & Brothers, 1952.

Athearn, Robert G. *American Heritage Illustrated History of the United States*, vol. 11, *The Gilded Age*. New York: Choice Publishing, 1988.

———. *American Heritage Illustrated History of the United States*, vol. 12, *A World Power*. New York: Choice Publishing, 1988.

Ayers, Edward L. *American Passages: A History of the United States*. Belmont, Calif.: Thomson Wadsworth, 2007.

Bailey, Thomas A. *The American Pageant*, 5th ed., vol. II. Lexington, Mass.: D. C. Heath, 1975.

Boardman, Fon W. Jr., *America and the Progressive Era, 1900–1917*. New York: Henry Z. Walck, 1970.

Commager, Henry Steele. *The American Destiny*, vol. 10, *The Rise of an Industrial Giant*. London: Orbis, 1986.

———. *The American Destiny*, vol.11, *Progress and Poverty*. London: Orbis, 1986.

Faragher, John Mack. *Out of Many: A History of the American People*. Upper Saddle River, N.J.: Prentice Hall, 1997.

Hanson, Erica. *A Cultural History of the United States: The 1920s*. San Diego, Calif.: Lucent Books, 1999.

Jeffrey, Julie, and Roy Jeffrey, eds. *The American People: Creating a Nation and Society*, 2nd ed. New York: HarperCollins, 1990.

Kazin, Michael. *The Populist Persuasion: An American History*. New York: BasicBooks, 1995.

Lord, Walter. *The Good Years: From 1900 to the First World War*. New York: Harper & Brothers, 1960.

May, Ernest R. *The Progressive Era*, vol. 9, *1901–1917*. New York: Time Incorporated, 1964.

Moquin, Wayne, ed. *Makers of America: The New Immigrants, 1904–1913.* New York: Encyclopaedia Britannica Educational Corporation, 1971.

Rosenbaum, Robert A. *The Penguin Encyclopedia of American History.* New York: Penguin Group, 2003.

Smith, Page. *America Enters the World: A People's History of the Progressive Era and World War I.* New York: McGraw-Hill, 1985.

Time-Life Books. *End of Innocence: 1910–1920.* Alexandria, Va.: Time-Life Books, 1998.

———. *Prelude to the Century.* Alexandria, Va.: Time-Life Books, 1998.

Uschan, Michael V. *A Cultural History of the United States: The 1910s.* San Diego, Calif.: Lucent Books, 1999.

Weinstein, Allen, and R. Jackson Wilson. *Freedom and Crisis: An American History.* New York: Random House, 1974.

FURTHER READING

Collier, Christopher, and James Lincoln Collier. *Progressivism, the Great Depression, and the New Deal, 1901–1941.* New York: Benchmark Books, 2001.

Halpern, Monica. *Progressives.* Washington, D.C.: National Geographic Society, 2003.

Link, Arthur Stanley. *Progressivism.* Wheeling, Ill.: Davidson, Harlan, 1983.

Sakany, Lois. *Platforms and Policies of America's Reform Politicians.* New York: Rosen Publishing Group, 2004.

Schneider, Dorothy. *American Women in the Progressive Era, 1900–1920.* New York: Facts on File, 1993.

Wingate, Katherine, and Kote Wingate. *Political Reforms: American Citizens Gain More Control Over Their Government.* New York: Rosen Publishing Group, 2004.

WEB SITES

The Legacy of Progressivism
http://www.tysknews.com/Depts/gov_philosophy/legacy_of_progressivism.htm.

Learn about the Progressive Era
http://www.digitalhistory.uh.edu/modules/progressivism/index.cfm.

Progressivism
http://www.prep.fairfield.edu/atschool/FacultyWebSites/rmauritz/progressivism.htm.
http://www.historyteacher.net/USProjects/USQuizzes/Progressivism1.htm.

Political Cartoons from the 1912 Presidential Election
http://www.archives.gov/education/lessons/election-cartoons/.

PICTURE CREDITS

INDEX

ABOUT THE AUTHOR

TIM McNEESE is associate professor of history at York College in York, Nebraska, where he is in his sixteenth year of college instruction. Professor McNeese earned an associate of arts degree from York College, a bachelor of arts in history and political science from Harding University, and a master of arts in history from Missouri State University. A prolific author of books for elementary, middle, and high school and college readers, McNeese has published more than 90 books and educational materials over the past 20 years, on everything from Picasso to landmark Supreme Court decisions. His writing has earned him a citation in the library reference work *Contemporary Authors*. In 2006, McNeese appeared on the History Channel program *Risk Takers/History Makers: John Wesley Powell and the Grand Canyon*. He was a faculty member at the 2006 Tony Hillerman Writers Conference in Albuquerque, New Mexico, where he presented on the topic of American Indians of the Southwest. Professor McNeese was a contributor to the 2007 *World Book Encyclopedia*.